Diabetes
Meals for
Good Health

SECOND EDITION

Includes Complete Meal Plans and **100** Recipes

Karen Graham, RD
Certified Diabetes Educator

Robert
ROSE

Diabetes Meals for Good Health
Text copyright © 2012, 2008 Durand & Graham, Ltd.
Photographs and illustrations copyright © 2012, 2008 Durand & Graham, Ltd.
Cover and text design copyright © 2012, 2008 Robert Rose Inc.

Some of the content of this book was previously published as *Meals for Good Health* (Paper Birch Publishing, 2007, 2005, 2003, 2001, 1998). *Meals for Good Health* has been translated into French and is published by Les Éditions de l'Homme in cooperation with Association Canadienne du Diabète, sold under the title *La santé au menu*, ISBN 978-2-7619-2785-7.

Disclaimer
The recipes in this book have been carefully tested by our kitchen and our tasters. To the best of our knowledge, they are safe and nutritious for ordinary use and users. For those people with food or other allergies, or who have special food requirements or health issues, please read the suggested contents of each recipe carefully and determine whether or not they may create a problem for you. All recipes are used at the risk of the consumer.

We cannot be responsible for any hazards, loss or damage that may occur as a result of any recipe use.

For those with special needs, allergies, requirements or health problems, in the event of any doubt, please contact your medical adviser prior to the use of any recipe.

Design: Durand & Graham, Ltd., with assistance from Steve Penner, Friesens Corporation
Production: Joseph Gisini/PageWave Graphics
Editors: Janice Madill, Easy English, and Sue Sumeraj
Proofreader: Sheila Wawanash
Indexer: Gillian Watts
Photographer: Brian Gould, Brian Gould Photography Inc.
Food Stylist: Judy Fowler
Cover Image: Colin Erricson, photographer; Kathryn Robertson, Food Stylist; Charlene Erricson, Prop Stylist
Image on Page 271: © iStockphoto.com/Mehmet Can
Hand Graphic Artwork: Sandi Storen

Cover image: Santa Fe Salad (see recipe, page 256)

Library and Archives Canada Cataloguing in Publication

Graham, Karen, 1959–
   Canada's diabetes meals for good health :
includes complete meal plans and 100 recipes /
Karen Graham. — 2nd ed.

Includes index.
ISBN 978-0-7788-0402-4

1. Diabetes—Diet therapy—Recipes. 2. Menus.
3. Cookbooks. I. Title.

RC662.G71 2012   641.5'6314   C2011-907406-0

Graham, Karen, 1959-
   Diabetes meals for good health :
includes complete meal plans and 100 recipes /
Karen Graham. — 2nd ed.

Includes index.
ISBN 978-0-7788-0403-1

1. Diabetes—Diet therapy—Recipes. 2. Menus.
3. Cookbooks I. Title.

RC662.G72 2012   641.5'6314   C2011-907404-4

We acknowledge the financial support of the Government of Canada through the Book Publishing Industry Development Program (BPIDP) for our publishing activities.

Published by Robert Rose Inc.
120 Eglinton Avenue East, Suite 800, Toronto, Ontario, Canada M4P 1E2
Tel: (416) 322-6552 Fax: (416) 322-6936
www.robertrose.ca

Printed and bound in Canada

6 7 8 9 TCP 20 19 18 17

Contents

Special Thanks

This book was first published almost 15 years ago under the title *Meals for Good Health*. Over the years, it has gone through many timely revisions, and it just keeps getting better! This edition features a unique new 32-page section, "Food Choices for Good Health," that rates food choices from healthy to unhealthy. I extend a huge thank you to Bob Dees, president of Robert Rose, who embraces the need for change and improvement. Bob understands the importance of this book as an essential tool to help you be healthier.

Thank you to the Canadian Diabetes Association for their partnership and commitment to helping people with diabetes. *Diabetes Meals for Good Health* brings us many steps closer to good health. My thanks to dietitian Barbara Selley and to Cathie Martin, who have methodically updated the nutritional analysis for all the recipes, meals and snacks. Also thanks to the dietitians of the Canadian Diabetes Association Materials Review Subcommittee: Nicole Aylward, Linda Mailhot-Hall, Beverley Harris, Rebecca Horsman, Michelle Knezic, Shari Segal and Sharon Zeiler.

As with any project, a large variety of people helped bring this latest edition together, and my thanks go to Marian Jarkovich and Nina McCreath at Robert Rose, as well as to editor Sue Sumeraj and to Joseph Gisini at PageWave Graphics. It was a pleasure to work with this knowledgeable and committed group.

The pictures look so good we want to eat the food right off the page! My huge thanks to the team of Brian Gould and Judy Fowler, photographer and food stylist extraordinaire, for the mouth-watering and realistic photographs. This book is a celebration of Brian and Judy's amazing skill and artistic talent.

The concept for this book was born following brainstorming and discussions with my husband, Rick Durand. Thank you, Rick, for your contribution of ideas, your reviews, your humor, your daily encouragement and love — you have been instrumental at every stage. Our children, Carl and Roslyn, grew up in the midst of the book and have gone on to be champions of healthy living. Thank you to my sister, Janice Madill, who has guided my writing of this book. And thanks to my parents, Marg and Bill Graham, for encouraging me to pursue my dream of becoming a dietitian.

This book is dedicated to my more than five thousand clients, who over the years were my inspiration to write this book.

How to Use This Book

Diabetes Meals for Good Health will help you make important changes to achieve good health.

Read through the first part of the book so that you understand how to use this book as a complete meal planner.

The book has beautiful life-size photographs that you will love to look at — yet it's a lot more than pictures and recipes. It is an effortless way to organize your daily calorie needs (from 1200 to 2200 calories) into delicious meals and snacks. I've counted all the calories for you, making it an easy-to-use daily meal planner. For each meal there are two photographs. The life-size photograph is the large meal and the small photograph is the small meal. You can see exactly how much food is the right portion for you. This first section of the book (pages 6–10) will show you how this works.

Karen Graham's Ten Changes for Good Health (pages 11–29)
Practical advice to help you feel better, lose weight and reduce your cholesterol, blood pressure and blood glucose. Start with one or two changes. When you are ready to make more changes, come back to this section and read it again.

Food Groups (pages 31–41)
After you read about the food groups you will understand how important it is to eat a variety of nutrient-rich food at each meal (as shown in the meal photographs in the book). Good nutrition prevents disease and is essential for good health.

Meals, Recipes and Snacks (pages 43–285)
There are 70 complete meals, 100 recipes and over 100 snacks for you to choose. Sections are color coded for ease of use (see page 6).

Food Choices for Good Health (pages 286–317)
Compare the calories, carbohydrates, fiber, fat and sodium in different cereals, egg breakfasts, soups, snacks, salads and more — 27 types of food in total. This will help you learn about food labels and healthier food choices.

Talk to your dietitian, diabetes educator or doctor
If you have questions along the way about your diet or diabetes, talk to a health professional.

5

Color Coded Sections of the Book

White	• How to Use This Book • Karen Graham's Ten Changes for Good Health • Food Groups
Yellow: *15 Breakfast Meals*	• All large meals have 370 calories • All small meals have 250 calories
Green: *15 Lunch Meals*	• All large meals have 520 calories • All small meals have 400 calories
Blue: *40 Dinner Meals*	• All large meals have 730 calories • All small meals have 550 calories
Purple: *4 Snack Groups*	• Low-calorie snacks have 20 calories or less • Small snacks have 50 calories • Medium snacks have 100 calories • Large snacks have 200 calories

Choose Your Meal Plan

This book shows large and small meals and different-sized snacks. This section will help you decide what meal size and how many snacks you will need.

Portions will be different for each member of your family. The small meals would be enough for most small children and older adults who are less active. Growing children and teenagers and physically active adults may need portions larger than even the large meals and large snacks. Children and teenagers, and pregnant and breastfeeding mothers, should include a cup of milk with each meal to meet their calcium needs.

To get an idea of the number of calories you need each day, do an Internet search on "energy requirements" or visit Health Canada's website or choosemyplate.gov.

There are two ways to help you choose your meal plan:
- Use the general rule.
- Use your hand size.

General Rule

If you are trying to lose weight, here is a general rule:
- Women choose 1,200–1,800 calories daily
- Men choose 1,500–2,200 calories daily

Use the Daily Meal Plan Chart on the next page to choose your meal plan.

Read this if you are on diabetes pills, insulin, heart pills or blood pressure pills

When you make changes, such as eating less or exercising more, you may not need as many pills or as much insulin. If you feel weak, shaky or dizzy when exercising, before meals or when getting out of bed, your medication may need to be adjusted. See your doctor. Do not change your pills or insulin without talking to your health-care professional first.

Weigh yourself no more than once a week

Your body weight goes up and down every day by one or two pounds, so it's not a good idea to weigh yourself every day. Weigh yourself just once a week, at the same time of day and in the same clothes, and you will notice a gradual weight loss. If you lose one or two pounds a month you are doing well, because these pounds will stay off.

If you do not have a weigh scale, have your doctor, dietitian or health worker weigh you at office visits.

If you are overweight by forty or fifty pounds or more, it probably took ten or more years to put that weight on. Expect to lose weight slowly; it is more likely that you will not regain it this way. Losing ten pounds in one year would be a great success for anyone.

Once you have estimated your daily calorie needs, you can choose your meal plan. Select a meal plan from the Daily Meal Plan Chart or make your own meal plan. You can mix and match your meals without ever worrying again about calories. Everything is worked out for you.

A. Daily Meal Plan Chart

• small meals with no snacks	1,200 calories
• small meals with two small snacks	1,300 calories
• small meals with one small and two medium snacks	1,450 calories
• small meals with one small, one medium and one large snack	1,550 calories
• large meals with no snacks	1,620 calories
• large meals with two small snacks	1,720 calories
• large meals with one small and two medium snacks	1,870 calories
• large meals with one small, one medium and one large snack	1,970 calories
• large meals with three large snacks	2,220 calories

B. Make Your Own Meal Plan

You can create your own meal plan for your calorie level. You can mix and match different sized meals and snacks, depending on the eating schedule that best fits your lifestyle. For example:

Meals & Snacks	Calories
Large breakfast	370
Small snack	50
Small lunch	400
Large snack	200
Large dinner	730
Medium snack	100
Total Calories	1,850

Calories for the small meals:

- breakfast has 250 calories
- lunch has 400 calories
- dinner has 550 calories

Calories for the large meals:

- breakfast has 370 calories
- lunch has 520 calories
- dinner has 730 calories

Calories for the snacks:

- low-calorie snack has 20 calories or less
- small snack has 50 calories
- medium snack has 100 calories
- large snack has 200 calories

Hand Size

- Go to page 114–115, to the life-size photograph of Dinner 1.
- If the palm of your hand is about the size of the 1½ chicken breasts and your fist is about the size of the 1½ potatoes, then choose the large meals.
- If the palm of your hand is closer in size to the one piece of chicken and your fist is about the size of the one potato, then the small meals are for you (shown in the small inset photograph).
- You may want to add several snacks to your daily meal plan. But if you are trying to lose weight, you may need to choose just the small snacks or the low-calorie snacks.
- Over time, based on your weight loss or gain, adjust the meal size and the number and size of snacks.

SMALL MEAL

Make the Meals and Recipes

All the book's 100 tested recipes are:

- easy to make
- low-cost and use common ingredients
- low in fat or sugar
- family favorites
- easy to freeze

Check the recipes for the number of servings. Some recipes will serve up to six people. If you live on your own, you may want to cut the recipes in half. If you are cooking for a large family, the recipes can be doubled. Leftovers can be safely kept in your fridge for three days, or frozen to be eaten later.

Measure your glasses and bowls

Your drinking glasses and cereal and soup bowls may be different shapes and sizes than the ones shown in the meal photographs. Fill up a measuring cup with water and pour the water into your glasses and bowls. Then you will know how much they hold.

Helpful Hint:

Choosing smaller glasses and dishes can help you reduce your portions.

 entertaining meal

At the end of each section, you'll find an entertaining meal (Breakfast 15, Lunch 15 and Dinner 40). These meals may take a bit longer to prepare or may have a few extra ingredients. But the calories are the same, so these special meals still fit perfectly in your meal plan.

Karen Graham's Ten Changes for Good Health

1. Eat Breakfast

2. Eat Proper Portions

3. Fill Up on Vegetables and Fruits

4. Eat Less Fat

5. Drink More Water

6. Limit Sugar

7. Limit Salt and Alcohol

8. Shop Smart

9. Limit Restaurant Meals

10. Walk for Health

1. Eat Breakfast

When you eat breakfast, you have more energy. Your body will "switch on" and start using up your fat. If you overeat in the evening when you are less active, your body will store fat.

Let me suggest two changes. First, start eating a small breakfast. Second, eat less in the evening.

2. Eat Proper Portions

Eat the portions outlined in the meals and snacks to get the number of calories and nutrients you need. Pages 7–9 will help you decide which portions are right for you.

Eat slowly to avoid overeating. Put down your fork, knife and spoon between bites. Drink water with your meals. Turn off the TV and focus on what you are eating. And save leftovers for the next meal.

Use smaller dishes and glasses
Your smaller portions of food will look like more on a smaller plate, and will be more satisfying.

The portion sizes and descriptions in the meals in this book are consistent with the ones you will find in Beyond the Basics: Meal Planning for Healthy Eating, Diabetes Prevention & Management *(Canadian Diabetes Association, 2007). In the meals here and in* Beyond the Basics, *you will see 60 mL used as the metric equivalent for ¼ cup. In the recipes, however, the standard recipe equivalent of 50 mL per ¼ cup is used.*

Small narrow glasses are your best choice

Does a 4- or 6-ounce (125 or 175 mL) glass of juice not seem like enough? Well, studies have shown that on average we will drink and eat the amount that is in front of us, and we can be just as satisfied with a smaller amount. With a measuring cup, check how much your drinking glasses hold and use the smaller glasses every day. Here, the glasses of apple juice don't really look that different, but the glass on the right holds *three times as much.* That means an extra 7 teaspoons (35 mL) of sugar!

4 ounces
60 calories

12 ounces
180 calories

3. Fill Up on Vegetables and Fruits

These foods are naturally low in fat and are full of fiber, vitamins and minerals. Especially fill up on low-calorie vegetables, listed on page 149.

If you eat more vegetables and fruit, you will find it easier to cut back on meats, fats, desserts and high-fat snack foods. This healthy balance of foods will fill you up, but not load you down with calories. **See next page for an example.**

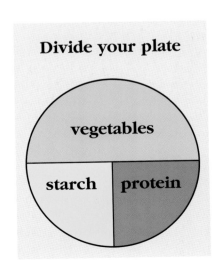

Divide your plate

vegetables

starch   protein

Divide your plate

Protein
¹⁄₄ of your plate;
such as lean meat,
chicken, fish,
beans or lentils

Starch
¹⁄₄ of your plate;
such as potatoes,
rice, pasta or bread

Vegetables
$\frac{1}{2}$ of your plate; try to have two kinds of vegetables

15

4. Eat Less Fat

Eating less fat is an important change to reduce blood cholesterol and keep your heart healthy, improve your diabetes and lower your risk for some kinds of cancer. Fat is high in calories, so cutting back also helps you lose weight. Particularly eat less of these unhealthy fats.

A few kinds of fats, called healthy fats, are beneficial to your heart (see page 41).

Unhealthy Fats

These fats need to be limited (but not totally avoided).

Saturated fat found in:
- lard, butter, and meat gravy
- meats such as beef, pork, lamb, skin-on chicken and turkey
- processed meats such as bacon, bologna, wieners, salami, sausages, liverwurst and canned meats
- eggs, high-fat hard cheese and cottage cheese, cream cheese, cream, high-fat sour cream and whole milk
- ice cream, chocolate, cookies and baked goods
- deep-fried foods and fast foods such as french fries, fried chicken, hamburgers and hot dogs
- coconut, coconut oil and palm oil

Cholesterol found in:
- most of the animal foods listed above
- liver and organ meats

Trans fats are man-made from vegetable oils and are found in:
- shortening and brick and hydrogenated margarine
- foods processed with hydrogenated and partially hydrogenated fat, such as french fries, potato chips, microwave popcorn, hydrogenated peanut butter, crackers, cookies and baked goods such as donuts
- smaller amounts, occurring naturally, in animal foods including beef, bologna, butter and milk fats

Moderation and portion control is the best message for good health

In *Diabetes Meals for Good Health,* meals that have higher amounts of saturated fat, trans fats or cholesterol are limited in portions and frequency so that your total fat intake is reasonable. For example, the meal plans encourage:
- small portions of meat or other protein
- low-fat dairy products such as skim milk
- small portions of desserts and snacks
- limited portions of spreads, regardless of whether you use margarine, butter or mayonnaise

Let's go on a grocery tour and look for hidden fat!

- Food labels list the amount of fat. Fat is listed in grams. Five grams (5 g) of fat is the same as 1 teaspoon (5 mL) of fat. On labels, serving sizes will vary. If one serving of three crackers has 5 g of fat, you will eat a whole teaspoon of fat when you eat those three crackers. That is a lot of hidden fat. A serving of three to five crackers with 2 g of fat or less would be a better choice.

- Foods labeled as *light* or *lite* may have less fat in them than the regular kinds. Compare the labels of the light kind with the regular one. Buy the one with the least amount of fat. For example, *light* hot chocolate usually has less fat and less sugar than regular hot chocolate. When a food is labeled as *light*, however, it may simply mean that the food is a light color. So check the label before you buy a food.

- *Low-fat* foods are often good choices. These foods have less vegetable fat and less animal fat than the regular brands. One serving of a low-fat food must have less than about half a teaspoon (2 mL) of fat (3 g). Look for low-fat mayonnaise, low-fat margarine and low-fat cheese.

- *Calorie-reduced* foods may also be good choices. They have fewer calories because they have less fat or sugar than the regular brand.

- One tablespoon (15 mL) of *fat-free* or *oil-free* salad dressing or *fat-free* sour cream has very little fat and very few calories. These are usually good choices.

- When a label says *trans-fat-free, no trans fat* or *cholesterol-free*, the food may still be high in vegetable fat and calories. For example, frozen french fries labeled *trans-fat-free* are made with vegetable oil and so are not low in fat. Remember, all types of animal fat and vegetable fat have the same high number of calories per gram.

*C*heck food labels — trans fats are unhealthy and are called:
- "hydrogenated vegetable oil"
- "hydrogenated palm oil"
- or may be listed as "partially hydrogenated" "vegetable shortening"

*C*heck the label and choose foods that are:
- low-fat
- calorie-reduced
- fat-free
- low-sugar
- light in calories

A food that has fewer than 10 calories in a serving is so low in calories that it will not have an effect on your weight.

Note: On a label, % M.F. (percent milk fat) or % B.F. (percent butter fat) tells you how much fat is in a food, such as milk or cheese. Choose the one with the lowest percent fat.

I suggest you try to avoid the bakeshop and the potato chip and cookie aisles when you go shopping.

The "Food Choices for Good Health" section on pages 286–317 has lots more tips on shopping and food labels.

- Let's look at the amount of fat in milk, and talk about what kinds of milk are best for most adults. In whole milk, half the calories come from fat. This is not a good choice, as we do not need all this fat. By choosing 2% milk, you will get less fat than in whole milk. In 1% milk, one-quarter of the calories still come from fat, so this is a better choice than 2% milk. Skim milk is fat-free, so it is the best choice for most adults. It may take time to get used to the new taste of skim milk, but it is a refreshing drink.

- Buy fewer fatty luncheon meats, such as salami and bologna, and sausages and bacon. Choose instead lean slices of ham, chicken, turkey or roast beef. A couple of the meals in this book do include a high-fat meat choice, such as wieners or sausages, but you'll see that because of the fat, the portions are small.

- Last on the shopping tour, we check the amount of fat and sugar in cookies, cakes and snacks. There are many low-fat crackers, such as soda crackers, melba toast and rice cakes. You may also be able to find baked snack foods with less added fat, for example, baked corn chips. These are better choices.

  All cookies and cakes have some fat and sugar. Arrowroot biscuits, social teas, digestive cookies and angel food cake are not as rich in fat as others.

  Some cookies or chocolate bars may be marked as *carbohydrate-reduced* or *sugar-free*. These may contain other sweeteners, such as sorbitol. They often have extra fat added to them, so may end up having more calories than the regular kind. Check the labels closely.

- Check the ingredients list on packaged foods. It is important to know that the first ingredients listed are the main ingredients. For example, if vegetable or palm oil is listed first, you will know the food is high in fat. If sugar, honey or glucose is listed first, this means the food is high in sugar.

18

More tips to help you eat less fat.

Add less fat to your food

Before you put butter, margarine, mayonnaise, cream or gravy on your food, ask yourself if you really need it. Try eating less of these fats. When you want a topping or spread, try a small amount of one of the low-fat or fat-free choices.

Take the fat off meat, chicken and fish

Trim the fat off meats, and take the skin off chicken, turkey or fish before cooking. Chicken or fish, cooked and eaten with the skin left on, can have just as much fat as fatty red meats.

Cook foods without adding fat

Many foods can be cooked in fat-free ways. Foods can be boiled, steamed, broiled or barbecued. Try steamed fish, broiled chicken or barbecued beef. If you occasionally want to fry foods, use a nonstick pan and don't add fat. Or cook in a heavy pan with some water or broth, or use a cooking spray, so the food doesn't stick to the pan.

Low-fat baking tip
Cut out at least half the fat called for in cake and muffin recipes.
To keep your muffins or cake moist, add a small amount of skim milk yogurt or applesauce, as in the muffin recipe on page 58.

Eat smaller portions of meat, chicken and fish

Now that you have cut off the extra fat and you are cooking without fat, you should try eating smaller portions of the meat, chicken and fish. Even if they are lean, they will still have hidden fat.

Try other flavorings on vegetables

Lightly cook your vegetables and they will be more tasty and healthful. Sprinkle them with lemon juice or spices instead of butter or margarine. A sprinkle of dill, parsley, pepper or garlic can really make your vegetables taste good.

Put less fat on your sandwiches

Spread your sandwiches with a small amount of salsa, mustard, relish or light mayonnaise instead of butter or margarine.

All fats have the same calories — whether lard, butter, margarine or oil.

Do you use butter or margarine?

Many people tell me that they use only 100% vegetable oil or margarine, with no cholesterol or trans fat. I agree these are better choices.

But remember, vegetable fats have the same number of calories as animal fats such as butter or lard. Fat is fattening, whether it's vegetable fat or animal fat. We need to eat less of all kinds of fats.

Many people believe bread and potatoes are fattening, so they cut down on these foods. Yet it is often the fats we add to the bread and potatoes that are fattening. So cut back on:

- the margarine you put on your bread
- the butter or sour cream you add to a baked potato
- eating potatoes as potato chips and french fries

A healthier choice is to reduce the fat we add to food — try a small or medium potato as part of a balanced meal topped with just 1 tablespoon (15 mL) of light sour cream and green onion tops for extra flavor.

Choose a variety of foods in the portions shown in *Diabetes Meals for Good Health* and you will get the right amount of fats and other nutrients — avoid the temptation to add loads of butter, margarine, or gravy to your foods.

*You are doing great.
Making changes takes time and
effort — but you are worth it!*

5. Drink More Water

Dietitians suggest drinking eight glasses of water a day. Eight glasses equals a two-quart (2 L) plastic soft drink bottle. Many of us get much of our water in our coffee, tea, juice or soft drinks each day. But our bodies don't need all the caffeine or sugar in these drinks. Feel free to drink some coffee, tea or diet soft drinks, but also drink lots of plain water. It is the best calorie-free drink.

Your body needs water to work properly. Water helps the body break down stored fat. Water helps keep you regular. Drinking water helps replace fluids when you exercise.

Here are some tips to help you start drinking more water.

Your need for water or other fluids increases in warm weather and with exercise. If you are a smaller body size, you may need only six glasses daily, whereas if you are a larger size, you may need more than eight glasses.

Remind yourself

Often we simply forget to drink water. If you like water cold, keep a bottle or jug of water in the fridge. Keep a water glass on your table or desk. When you see the jug or glass, you will remember to drink water.

Drink water in the morning

We are naturally thirsty when we first wake up. Drink water first thing in the morning.

Drink water with meals

Get into the habit of drinking water with all your meals and snacks. Add a slice of lemon to your water for a fresh taste.

Drink water whenever you feel hungry

Water fills your stomach so you feel full and eat less.

***Water makes life flow.
Go with the flow.***

6. Limit Sugar

Sugar is found naturally in fruits, vegetables and even milk. Starches found in breads and cereals change into sugar after you eat them. The sugar in these foods gives you energy. These foods also have many other nutrients. These foods are good for you in the amounts shown in the meals and snacks.

We need to limit pure sugars — white sugar, brown sugar, icing sugar, corn syrup, maple syrup, molasses and honey. One type of pure sugar is not better nor worse than another. These pure sugars give us calories we don't need and very little nutrition. Such sugars are called "empty calories."

Different cereals have different amounts of sugar:

Bran flakes have a small amount of sugar added (1 tsp/5 mL or 4 g in ³/₄ cup/175 mL).

Frosted flakes have a large amount of sugar added (3 tsp/15 mL or 12 g in ³/₄ cup/175 mL).

See page 292 for more information.

Sugars are added to most processed foods. In fact, it is hard to find a food label without sugar on the ingredient list. If sugar is the first ingredient, it means the food has more sugar than anything else. Try to limit sugary foods.

Lots of sugar can be found in what you drink. High-sugar drinks include fruit drinks, fruit crystal drinks, fruit juice, regular soft drinks, sweetened crushed ice drinks, chocolate milk, milk shakes and cappuccinos. One cup (250 mL) of unsweetened fruit juice or 1 cup of regular soft drink has about 7 teaspoons (35 mL) of sugar. Choose water or diet drinks instead.

You may see words such as "sucrose," "fructose," "sorbitol" and "mannitol" on food labels. Sucrose and fructose are pure sugars and they are not low-calorie. Sorbitol and mannitol are types of sugars, called "sugar alcohols," that have fewer calories than table sugar. They raise the blood sugar more slowly, but may cause gas.

*Sucrose, fructose, sorbitol and mannitol are **not** low-calorie sweeteners.*

Cookies, candies and chocolates made with sorbitol are often high in fat and calories. In fact, they may have similar or more calories than the regular cookies, candies or chocolates, so should be limited.

7. Limit Salt and Alcohol

Limit salt

Salt gives us sodium, an important mineral. Sodium occurs naturally in foods and is added to most processed foods. For good health, you need only a small amount of sodium — less than 2,300 mg per day. This is the amount in about 1 teaspoon (5 mL) of salt.

Unfortunately, most of us get more salt than we need. We eat too many salty processed foods and many of us add too much salt to our food. This extra salt in our diet makes extra work for our kidneys.

Cutting back on salt is a good healthy change for everyone. If you have high blood pressure, cutting back on salt may help reduce your blood pressure. Cutting back on salt means eating fewer processed foods, shaking a little less salt on your food, adding less salt (or no salt) to your recipes and limiting salty foods.

Other important dietary changes are cutting back on fat and alcohol, and choosing foods from the different food groups (see pages 31–41). Potassium, found in fruits and vegetables, is especially good for you. Making other changes including losing weight (if you are overweight), exercising, quitting smoking, and reducing your stress are important for reducing blood pressure (and reducing cholesterol). It is also important to take your medication as advised by your doctor and have your blood pressure checked regularly.

Try these tips to cut back on salt:
- Season your food during cooking and at the table with spices and herbs, lemon juice, lime juice or vinegar.
- Use pepper instead of salt.
- Use garlic powder or onion powder instead of garlic salt or onion salt. Try the Spice Mix on page 141 or the Seasoned Bread Crumbs on page 148.
- Use less salt in cooking and baking. For many recipes you don't need to add any salt.
- Look for low-sodium or unsalted foods, such as unsalted soda crackers.
- Choose fresh or frozen vegetables instead of canned.
- Eat fewer frozen, take-out and restaurant meals. They are generally high in salt and fat.

Iodine
Iodized salt provides us with iodine. Iodine is essential to keep your thyroid healthy. The thyroid regulates how you burn calories. A small amount of iodized salt gives you all the iodine you need. Ocean water fish and shellfish are some of the best natural food sources of iodine.

Once you start to cut back on salt, you will notice that many processed and restaurant foods begin to taste too salty. At the grocery store, be sure to check the amount of sodium per serving on the Nutrition Facts label.

See pages 286–317 to learn more about cutting back on salt.

Salt in *Diabetes Meals for Good Health* recipes:

- Salt is not added to the recipes unless needed for rising or recipe quality.
- The flavor of some of the recipes is enhanced by the salt found in the bouillon powder, soy sauce or seasoning salt. If you need to cut out more salt, then instead use more spices and herbs and reduced-salt products.

The meals include some salty foods, such as dill pickles, sauerkraut, sausages, ham and wieners. In the portions shown, these foods can be part of a healthy diet if eaten occasionally (once or twice a month).

If you need to cut out more of your salt, then you could choose:

- sliced cucumber instead of a dill pickle
- plain cabbage instead of sauerkraut
- unsalted beef or pork instead of sausages or wieners
- leftover cooked meat or chicken, or an egg instead of processed meat on sandwiches

Limit alcohol

One beer or two ounces of hard liquor, such as whisky or rum, has about the same number of calories as two slices of bread.

Six beers have 900 calories, equal in calories to about a loaf of bread. That's a lot. Six diet soft drinks have only 20 calories.

* For more information on alcohol and diabetes, please visit www.diabetes.org or www.diabetes.ca.

If you want to lose weight, you must look at everything you eat and drink, including alcohol. **Alcohol is high in calories.** Like sugar, alcohol is full of "empty calories." In this book you will find a glass of wine as an option with one of the meals. A light beer and an ounce of whisky are shown in the snack photographs as occasional choices only. **Daily intake of alcohol should be only on the advice of your doctor.**

The calories in hard liquor, such as whisky, come from the alcohol alone. Three-quarters of the calories in beer comes from the alcohol with the rest coming mostly from sugar. In liqueurs, just over half the calories come from alcohol and the rest come from sugar.

To reduce calories from alcoholic drinks:

- Drink less beer, wine, liqueurs and hard liquor. Instead drink water, diet beverages, no-alcohol low-calorie beer, or coffee or tea.
- Choose a light or extra-light beer, which has less sugar and less alcohol than regular beer.
- Instead of drinking a whole beer, have just half a beer and mix it with diet ginger ale.
- Most of the no-alcohol beers and no-alcohol wines have sugar (though usually less sugar than soft drinks) but are still a better choice than beer that has alcohol.
- If you want to have a glass of wine, choose dry wine. This has less sugar than sweet wine.
- Avoid liqueurs, which are heavy on alcohol and sugar.
- If you choose to have a drink of hard liquor, mix it with a diet soft drink or water, instead of juice or regular soft drinks.
- Drink water before and with your meals, instead of alcohol. Alcohol often makes you feel hungrier.

Caution:
- *Alcohol is not recommended for children and teenagers, and women who are pregnant or breastfeeding.*
- *Always talk to your doctor or the pharmacist about how your medications react with alcohol.*
- *If you have diabetes and take insulin or diabetes pills, drinking alcohol can cause a low blood glucose reaction. To avoid this problem, don't drink; or limit your drinks to one or two, and have something to eat with your drink.*

Alcohol is more than just a source of calories, it is an addictive drug. If you drink too much alcohol, it will affect more than your weight. Alcohol will make it hard to make other changes in your life.

Drinking less alcohol or quitting drinking is a difficult choice but help is available.

Think about making a change.

8. Shop Smart

You'll find lots of shopping tips on pages 286–317.

Plan your shopping trip carefully; use a list so you buy healthy foods. If you are hungry when you go grocery shopping, you will be easily tempted to buy the high-fat and high-sugar snacks. Try to go shopping after you've had something to eat. Remember, whatever you buy, you or your family will eat. You don't need to buy more cookies, ice cream and chips, just because you've eaten them all up.

9. Limit Restaurant Meals

I suggest that you limit restaurant meals. Restaurant meals are often large portions and high in fat, sugar and salt. The month of meals in this book shows you just a few restaurant meals. These meals can also be made at home.

10. Walk for Health

It is very important to keep active. Experts recommend about thirty minutes of exercise a day. For people with diabetes, a minimum of 150 minutes per week is recommended. If half an hour is too long for you, instead go for three ten-minute walks a day.

Walking is one of the best kinds of exercise. You can walk when you want and where you want. Start off slowly and try walking a little faster and further each week.

Walking is the best exercise for most of us.

Most of the people I counsel say they are active. I tell them that there is a difference between being active (or busy) and exercising. I compare the way we live today with the lives of our grandparents. People used to walk to work, to the store, to the post office, to school, to church and to the dance hall. Working in the home and on the farm was hard exercise. Today, we don't walk enough. We sit or stand for hours a day, whether at home or at work. Television and computers too often replace active play and work. This lack of exercise makes us unhealthy.

Are you simply too tired to go for a walk? When your muscles are weak, you will feel tired. It may seem strange, but the only way to have the energy for walking is to go for a walk. Once you become more fit, you will find that walking gives you energy.

*You will find that exercise **gives** you more energy.*

Are you so busy you can't find the time to go for a walk? Finding the time for a walk means making a few changes. Think about how often you go outside to do something — such as start the car or go to the bus stop, or get the mail. Once you are outside, take an extra twenty minutes to go for a walk. Walking is an important part of keeping healthy. We usually can find the time to do things we think are important.

It is a dream to think you can lose weight without regular exercise. Walking can help you lose weight, regulate your blood glucose and help you look and feel better. Walking keeps your bones and muscles strong. You will breathe deeper and easier. Walking often reduces back pain and other joint pain. Walking can help you reduce your stress and help you sleep better at night.

Walking helps you lose weight and helps you in many other ways.

*Walking outdoors is a great way to get some vitamin D. When your skin is exposed to sunlight, your body makes vitamin D. If you are Caucasian (lighter skinned), cover up or use a sunscreen for outdoor walks longer than about 20 minutes. **Avoid** the hottest time of day, sun tanning and sun burns.*

If you have diabetes, walking helps you lower your blood sugar. If you have high blood cholesterol, walking helps you lower your blood cholesterol. If you have high blood pressure, walking will help bring it down.

When I see a client two months after they have started walking, they tell me they feel healthier. They have often lost weight. They have more energy and are now ready to do more exercise, as it gets easier with each passing day.

It may take several months to get into a walking routine. Once you start walking regularly, you will feel better.

Put this book down and go for a walk.

Here are some helpful walking tips

First, start walking more each day.

When you go shopping, park at the far end of the lot and walk. When you take the bus, get off one stop early and walk that extra block.

Walking up and down stairs is great exercise. Start by walking down stairs.

Comfortable shoes or boots that fit well and give your feet good support are important.

Then, start walking as a regular exercise.

Try to go for a walk twice a week. It may help to walk at the same time each day so it becomes a habit — a good habit. Your dog would love to go for a walk any time. Watching TV wastes good walking time.

Boldly mark your calendar after each walk, and feel proud of yourself.

Mark your calendar each day you go for a walk.

Next, walk further. Walk more often. Walk faster and swing your arms.

Walk faster and further and you will lose more weight.

Now that you are walking, you may decide to also do some swimming, biking or dancing. Using an exercise bike or a treadmill are also excellent ways to exercise.

Walking takes time, but it gives you a lifetime of better health. Enjoy!

Good Sources of Fiber

Food Groups

Grains & Starches

Start with Grains and Starches

Grains and starches such as wheat, oats, corn, rice, potatoes, lentils, beans and cassava are the staple foods for most people around the world. Grains and starches are made into breakfast cereals and are ground into flour to make breads, pitas, tortillas, noodles, bannocks and rotis.

Grains and starches provide energy, are low in fat and are low in cost. They are bulk foods that help us feel full. Starches add vitamins and minerals to our diet. The energy we obtain from starchy foods is the preferred source of energy for our brain, muscles and nerves.

Whole-grain foods, such as whole wheat or rye bread, barley or oatmeal, contain fiber. Fiber is a natural laxative. It may help reduce your risk for colon cancer and help lower your blood cholesterol and blood glucose. Fiber helps you feel full and can help you lose weight.

The North American diet has changed over the last century. We now eat fewer grains and starches and we eat more meat and processed foods. Processed foods have added fat, sugar and salt. We suffer from diseases such as diabetes, heart disease and cancer that are linked to these changes in food choices.

We need to eat less meat, fat and processed food. Then starches and vegetables can start filling up more of our plate (see pages 13–15).

You will find that all the meals in *Diabetes Meals for Good Health* include grains and starches, with little or no added fat. Low-fat starch foods are also good for snacks.

How much starch should you eat at your meals?
- *Have a starch food with every meal.*
- *Size of your fist for each meal.*

Vegetables & Fruits

Fill Up on Vegetables and Fruits

Fresh or frozen vegetables and fruits are the best. Check the label and choose frozen ones that do not have salt, fat or sugar added.

Fruit canned in water or juice is a better choice than fruit canned in syrup. If canned in juice or syrup, drain off most of the juice. Choose these less often.

Juices

You may be surprised to learn that "unsweetened" fruit juices have sugar. One cup (250 mL) of unsweetened apple, orange or grapefruit juice has 6 to 7 teaspoons (30 to 35 mL) of natural sugar. Grape and prune juice have almost 10 teaspoons (50 mL) of sugar in a cup. Since juice has less fiber and is not as filling as fresh fruit, it is easy to drink too much. If you drink a lot of juice, it will be harder for you to lose weight. If you have diabetes, fruit juices may cause your blood glucose to go too high.

Vegetable juices, such as tomato juice, have less sugar than fruit juices, but often more salt. Several meals include a small glassful. When you are thirsty, drink water, not juices.

Dried fruit has more sugar than fresh fruit because the water has been taken out. For example, 2 tablespoons (25 mL) of raisins has 4 teaspoons (20 mL) of sugar; about the same amount of sugar as ½ cup (125 mL) of grapes.

Many of the lunches and dinners shown have two or more vegetables. This may be more than you are used to eating. It is an important change. Most of the breakfasts include fruit. Fruit is often the dessert for lunch or dinner.

When you are hungry between meals, eating a vegetable or a fruit would be better than eating a high-fat snack food or a rich dessert. You will find a variety of snack choices on pages 278–285.

Vegetables and fruits give you energy. They are low in fat. They add vitamins, minerals and extra fiber to your diet. They help reduce your risk for cancer.

How many vegetables and fruits should you eat?
- *Include a fruit with breakfast.*
- *Include two or more vegetables at lunch and dinner, and a fruit if you'd like.*
- *Choose a fruit or vegetable for a snack.*
- *Hold your two hands together and overfill them with vegetables and you will have a good daily amount.*

Calcium-Rich Foods

Choose Milk and Calcium-Rich Foods

Calcium is a mineral that makes your bones and teeth strong. It is found in milk and foods made from milk, such as yogurt and cheese. Calcium is also found in other foods, such as dried beans and soft fish bones. Vitamin D helps calcium work, and is found in fatty fish and is added to milk and some milk products.

Infants and growing children need extra calcium as their bones and teeth grow. Many people believe that milk and other calcium foods are just for kids. The truth is, we need calcium all our adult life to keep our bones strong.

Does drinking milk give you stomach pains? If so, you may not be able to fully digest the natural sugar (lactose) in the milk. You may find you are able to digest small amounts of milk or foods made from milk, such as cheese or yogurt. You could also drink lactose-reduced skim milk.

You can get your daily calcium from other foods, such as:
- tofu made with added calcium (check the label)
- soy or rice drinks and fruit juice made with added calcium
- beans, such as baked beans
- seeds and nuts, such as almonds and sesame seeds
- fish bones, such as those in canned salmon
- dark green, leafy vegetables, such as broccoli, Brussels sprouts, okra, kale and Chinese cabbage
- a few fruits, such as dried figs and oranges

Choose low-fat, calcium-rich foods, such as:
- low-fat milk, low-fat yogurt (skim or 1%) and low-fat cheeses (less than 20% milk fat)
- skim milk powder
- salmon canned in water, not oil (mash in the bones)
- low-fat soy milk (some have extra sugar added)
- dark green, leafy vegetables and beans are naturally low in fat

Seeds, nuts and tofu have vegetable fat; they can be chosen in the amounts shown in the meals.

Most of the meals in *Diabetes Meals for Good Health* include one or more calcium-rich foods. You'll also find a variety of calcium-rich foods in the snack section.

How much milk and calcium-rich food should you eat?
- *At every meal, try to include one or two low-fat calcium-rich foods.*
- *For a serving, have $\frac{1}{2}$ to 1 cup (125 to 250 mL) of milk or yogurt, $\frac{1}{4}$ to $\frac{1}{2}$ cup (60 to 125 mL) of canned fish with bones, or a thumb-size amount of a solid food like cheese, nuts or tofu.*

milk

cheese

Meats & Other Proteins

Eat the Right Amount of Protein

Proteins are important to keep you healthy. However, we need only a small amount of protein every day. The meals in this book show you how much protein to eat.

Protein is found in meat, fish, poultry, eggs, cheese and milk, and in alternative sources such as legumes (beans, peas and lentils), tofu and peanut butter. Nuts, seeds and many vegetables and grains also supply protein. I have included a variety of vegetable and animal proteins in the meals.

Vegetable proteins

Kidney beans, brown beans, chickpeas and dried peas are low-fat, high-fiber vegetable proteins. Tofu is made from soy beans and can replace meat. Smaller amounts of vegetable protein are found in starchy foods, such as whole-grain breads and oatmeal.

Nuts, including peanuts or peanut butter, and seeds, such as sunflower seeds, are high-fat non-meat proteins. They can still be a good choice for some meals and snacks, in the right amounts.

Animal proteins

Lean red meats are a good choice for low-fat animal protein. They include lean hamburger, and fat-trimmed round roast or steak, loin lamb or pork chop, and deer or rabbit. Chicken and turkey are a good source of protein, but remember to remove the skin.

Eggs are a good source of protein. Do you ask, "Can I eat eggs with high blood cholesterol?" Yes, you can safely eat up to three eggs a week. There are other important ways to reduce your high blood cholesterol (see pages 23 and 28).

Fish with the skin taken off has less fat than most red meat. Some of the best low-fat fish are ocean perch, red snapper, cod, haddock and sole. Light tuna, pink salmon and sardines canned in water are good choices too. Shrimp and lobster are also low in fat. Bluefish is a medium-fat fish. The fattier fishes are lake trout or red (sockeye) salmon; eat smaller portions of these. Try to eat fish at least twice a week; they are the best source of healthy omega-3 fat.

In general, you will find protein foods in the American Diabetes Association's Meat and Meat Substitutes Exchange Group and in the Canadian Diabetes Association's Meat & Alternatives Food Group.

You need only a small amount of protein each day.

How much protein should you eat?
- *Size of the palm of your hand for your main meal; half or less at your other two meals.*
- *For women, this usually means about 3 to 5 ounces (90 to 150 g) of cooked meat or other protein, and for men, about 4 to 7 ounces (125 to 210 g) at the main meal.*

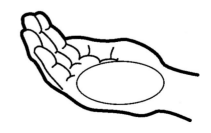

Foods Rich in Healthy Fats

Include Some Healthy Fats

Good Choices

Polyunsaturated fat and monosaturated fats found in:

- vegetable oils such as canola, olive, peanut, corn, safflower, sunflower and flaxseed oil
- soft tub non-hydrogenated margarines or salad dressings made from these oils
- avocados, olives and olive oil are rich in monounsaturated fats; these fats can help reduce blood cholesterol
- nuts such as walnuts, almonds, hazelnuts, pecans, peanuts and pistachios
- seeds such as sunflower, sesame and flaxseeds

Best Choices

Omega-3 polyunsaturated fat is healthy for your brain and eyes. Research shows it may lower your risk for heart attacks and stroke because it lowers triglycerides (blood fat) and helps keep the blood from clotting.

Fish, especially cold water ocean fish, is the best source of omega-3 fats. Fish can also contain some omega-6 fat, monounsaturated fat or smaller amounts of saturated fat. Fish is rich in selenium, B vitamins and vitamin D. I recommend eating fish as part of a healthy diet. Due to pollution in fresh and salt water, if you are pregnant, check with your doctor before regularly including fish in your diet.

Omega-3 fat is found in:

- sardines, salmon, trout, bass, mackerel, herring, anchovies,sturgeon, halibut and tuna
- shellfish such as shrimp, lobster, clams, oysters, mussels and snow crab
- ground flaxseed or flaxseed oil and pumpkin seeds
- non-hydrogenated canola oil or soybean oil, or the margarines or salad dressings made from these oils
- walnuts
- omega-3 fortified products such as eggs, yogurt, milk and cheese (check for omega-3 on labels)
- soy nuts, soybeans, soy flour or wheat germ
- purslane, *Portulaca oleracea;* this plant is known as a garden "weed" yet is a source of omega-3 fat

*L*imit "Unhealthy Fats"; see page 16.

A serving of olives, nuts or seeds, avocado or ground flax is the amount that fits in the small part of your palm.

How much fat should you eat at each meal?
- *The added fat should not be bigger than the tip of your thumb (1 to 2 tsp/5 to 10 mL).*
- *This includes fat added during cooking as well as at the table.*

Food Choices and Nutrient Values

With each large and small meal in this book, you will see a table of Food Choices, together with total carbohydrate and fiber. And with each recipe, you will find a table of nutrients per serving.

The Food Choices for the meals are based on the portions described in the *Canadian Diabetes Association Beyond the Basics* poster and manual. *Exception:* When a meal includes an accompanying recipe, one Carbohydrate choice is assigned per 15 g of available carbohydrate. On page 50, for example, 33 g of available carbohydrate in three pancakes is counted as 2 Carbohydrate choices. The nutrient values for each choice type (Carbohydrate, Fat, and Meat and Alternatives) are shown in the table below.

Comparing Carbohydrate Choices with Available Carbohydrate

You may notice that the Carbohydrate choices for a meal are sometimes not exactly equivalent to the total available carbohydrate. There are a couple of reasons for this.

1. Choices based on *Beyond the Basics* generally do not include carbohydrate from vegetables and miscellaneous sources such as nuts, seeds and condiments. As a result, Carbohydrate choices assigned to meals containing these foods (especially vegetables) will not account for all the available carbohydrate.

2. On the other hand, the Carbohydrate choices may account for slightly more than the total available carbohydrate. This happens because not all food choices in a group have exactly the same nutrients and because food choice counts are rounded.

These differences generally balance each other out. However, if you are counting carbohydrates, it's a good idea to note the total carbohydrate and fiber values.

Calculation of Nutrient Values

Nutrient values for the recipes and meals, and items in the "Food Choices for Good Health" section, were calculated by Food Intelligence (Toronto, Ontario) with the assistance of Genesis R&D software, using the Canadian Nutrient File and USDA Nutrient Database for Standard Reference. The calculations were based on the common weights and measures (teaspoons, tablespoons, cups, pounds, etc.) and the following standard ingredients and/or quantities:

- skim milk
- lean ground beef (hamburger) containing less than 17% fat;
- rice and pasta without the addition of salt;
- 3 medium or 4 small boiling potatoes per pound (500 g), and approximately 3 large or 4 medium baking potatoes per 2 pounds (1 kg);
- granulated white sugar unless otherwise specified; and
- typical additions of unmeasured ingredients (e.g. tomato in sandwich).

If there was a choice of ingredients, the first listed was calculated. If there was a range of quantity, the smaller amount was calculated.

Food Choices	NUTRIENTS PER CHOICE		
	Available carbohydrate	Protein	Fat
Carbohydrates			
Grains & Starches	15 g	3 g	0 g
Fruits	15 g	1 g	0 g
Milk & Alternatives	15 g	8 g	variable
Other Choices	15 g	variable	variable
Vegetables (usually not counted)	<5 g (most)	2 g	0 g
Fat	0 g	0 g	5 g
Meat and Alternatives	0 g	7 g	3–5 g

Available carbohydrate = total carbohydrate minus fiber.

For additional information about diet and diabetes, visit
- www.diabetes.org
- www.diabetes.ca

Meals, Recipes and Snacks

Breakfast Meals

- **each large breakfast has 370 calories**
- **each small breakfast has 250 calories**

BREAKFAST 1

Dry Cereal

For a list of healthy nut choices, see page 41.

As an alternative to nuts, you could top your cereal with ¼ cup (60 mL) (or 2 tbsp/25 mL for the small meal) of Crunchy Nut Granola (see page 70). This choice would have similar calories to the nuts, but more carbohydrates.

Look at the cereal labels before you buy. Choose cereals that have little or no added sugar. One serving should have less than 5 grams of sugar and less than 2 grams of fat.

If a cereal is made with added dried fruit, such as raisins, it will have a higher amount of sugar. For example, 1 tablespoon (15 mL) of raisins adds an extra 5 grams of sugar. If you are choosing a cereal with added fruit, you should have a smaller portion of fruit on the side.

Another thing to look for when you buy cereals is fiber. Cereals with a lot of fiber are a good choice. These would include bran cereals and whole wheat cereals. Check the label for the amount of fiber per serving.

Skim milk and 1% milk have very little fat, and are the best choice for your cereal and for drinking. If you use canned milk, buy skim evaporated milk. Remember, ¼ cup (60 mL) evaporated milk mixed with ¼ cup (60 mL) water is the same as ½ cup (125 mL) regular milk.

Add fruit to your cereal or eat it on the side. Choose ½ a large banana or any of the fruits you see with the other breakfast meals. A half-cup (125 mL) of unsweetened juice has the same calories as one small fruit, but it does not have the fiber. The nuts topping your cereal add a source of protein and healthy fats.

Drink water with all your meals, including breakfast. If you have a cup of coffee or tea, go easy on the sugar. Cut it out if you can, or use a low-calorie sweetener. Also, go easy on the cream and coffee whitener. You probably know that cream has a lot of fat, but did you know that coffee whitener is made mostly with sugar and oil? Instead of using cream or coffee whitener, try using skim milk or skim milk powder. If you want to use coffee whitener, buy the light kind and limit yourself to a couple of teaspoons a day.

Food Choices	Large Meal	Small Meal
Carbohydrate	3½	3
Fat	2	1
Nutritional Info	**Large Meal**	**Small Meal**
Carbohydrate	60 g	48 g
Fibre	10 g	7 g

Your Breakfast Menu	Large Meal (370 calories)	Small Meal (250 calories)
Bran flakes cereal	1 cup (250 mL)	¾ cup (175 mL)
Skim or 1% milk	1 cup (250 mL)	1 cup (250 mL)
½ large banana	3-inch (7.5-cm) piece	3-inch (7.5-cm) piece
Sliced almonds or other nuts	3 tbsp (45 mL)	1½ tbsp (22 mL)

SMALL MEAL

BREAKFAST 2

Egg & Toast

In the morning, we all need good food to get our brains going!

For your toast, choose whole-grain bread, such as whole wheat or rye bread. These breads have a lot of fiber.

For a light choice, put a small amount of jam or honey on your toast, without butter or margarine.

Boil an egg, or poach or fry it in a nonstick pan with no added fat. Choose eggs that have been enriched with omega-3 fats to boost your heart health.

Large eggs have almost the same yolk size as small eggs. Large eggs are larger because they have more egg white. This means that a small egg has about the same cholesterol as a large egg.

Drink ½ cup (125 mL) of skim milk or 1% milk with this meal; ½ cup (125 mL) of buttermilk is also low in fat.

A small serving of fruit or several slices of tomato goes with this meal. For a change, try ½ cup (125 mL) of tomato or vegetable juice. Tomato juice would be a light choice since it has half the sugar of fruit juice.

A note about fruit juice:
Fresh fruit is a better choice than fruit juice. This is because fresh fruit has more fiber and is more filling. However, you can choose ½ cup (125 mL) of unsweetened orange juice instead of one small orange.

Sugar, honey or jam have fewer calories than butter or margarine. This is because a gram of sugar has fewer calories than a gram of fat.
- *1 teaspoon (5 mL) of sugar, honey or regular jam or jelly has 20 calories.*
- *1 teaspoon (5 mL) of butter or margarine has about 45 calories.*

Food Choices	Large Meal	Small Meal
Carbohydrate	3	2
Meat and Alternatives	1	1
Fat	1	1
Nutritional Info	Large Meal	Small Meal
Carbohydrate	51 g	35 g
Fiber	6 g	4 g

Your Breakfast Menu	Large Meal (370 calories)	Small Meal (250 calories)
Egg (cooked without fat)	1	1
Brown toast	2 slices	1 slice
Margarine	1 tsp (5 mL)	—
Jam or jelly	1 tsp (5 mL)	1 tsp (5 mL)
Skim or 1% milk	½ cup (125 mL)	½ cup (125 mL)
Orange slices	½ medium orange	½ medium orange

SMALL MEAL

BREAKFAST 3

Pancakes & Bacon

These thin pancakes are easy to make. They are lower in fat and sugar than the store-bought pancake mixes.

Syrup replaces fruit in this breakfast.

Cook your bacon until crisp. Reduce the fat by draining off the grease. One thin slice of lean ham, back bacon or turkey bacon has less fat than the slice of bacon shown. Because bacon is higher in saturated fat and sodium, choose it no more than once a week.

Look at the labels on light syrup. Two tablespoons (25 mL) should have fewer than 60 calories. Two tablespoons (25 mL) of this light syrup are the same as 1 tablespoon (15 mL) of most regular syrups.

For extra fiber, add 1 tablespoon (15 mL) of bran to your batter.

If you don't have a nonstick pan, coat your frying pan lightly with a greased paper towel, or use a cooking spray.

Low-Fat Pancakes

Makes sixteen 4-inch (10 cm) pancakes

1½ cups (375 mL) flour

½ tsp (2 mL) salt

1 tsp (5 mL) baking powder

1 tbsp (15 mL) sugar

1 egg

1 tbsp (15 mL) oil, margarine or butter, melted

1¾ cups (425 mL) skim milk

Per pancake	
Calories	67
Carbohydrate	11 g
Fiber	0 g
Protein	3 g
Fat, total	1 g
Fat, saturated	0 g
Cholesterol	12 mg
Sodium	107 mg

1. In a large bowl, mix together the flour, salt, baking powder and sugar.
2. In a medium bowl, beat the egg with a fork. Add the fat and milk to the egg, and mix well.
3. Add the egg mixture to the flour mixture. Stir until smooth. It helps to stir with a wire whisk. If it is too thick add a little more milk.
4. Cook in a nonstick pan, on medium heat, or in an electric nonstick pan. Use just under ¼ cup (50 mL) of batter for each pancake. Once the pancakes have small bubbles, turn them over.

Food Choices	Large Meal	Small Meal
Carbohydrate	3½	2½
Fat	2	1½
Nutritional Info	**Large Meal**	**Small Meal**
Carbohydrate	57 g	38 g
Fiber	1 g	1 g

Your Breakfast Menu	Large Meal (370 calories)	Small Meal (250 calories)
Low-Fat Pancakes	3	2
Syrup	1½ tbsp (22 mL), or 3 tbsp (45 mL) light syrup	1 tbsp (15 mL), or 2 tbsp (25 mL) light syrup
Bacon, crisp	2 strips	1½ strips

SMALL MEAL

BREAKFAST 4

Toast & Peanut Butter

This simple breakfast has protein to start your day. One tablespoon (15 mL) of peanut butter is a good source of protein. But peanut butter has a lot of fat, so put it on a dry piece of toast — you don't need to add extra fat.

Half an apple is served with this breakfast.

Here are a few examples of other fruit servings:
- $\frac{1}{2}$ cup (125 mL) of unsweetened applesauce
- 2 medium kiwis
- $\frac{1}{4}$ of a small melon
- 1 small banana
- 1 orange
- $\frac{1}{2}$ grapefruit. See Breakfast 8 for a new way to enjoy grapefruit.

In place of the $\frac{1}{2}$ cup (125 mL) of milk, you may have 1 cup (250 mL) of light hot cocoa (see Breakfast 9).

For the large meal, try the peanut butter on your first piece of toast and 1 teaspoon (5 mL) of jam or jelly on your second piece of toast.

Jams — Regular or Diet
A light (or "diet") jam or jelly should have fewer than 10 calories in 1 teaspoon (5 mL) (30 calories in 1 tablespoon/15 mL). Two teaspoons (10 mL) of this light jam are about the same as 1 teaspoon (5 mL) of regular jam or jelly.

Jams marked "no sugar added" may in fact have added sugar in the form of concentrated fruit juice. These jams often have almost the same amount of carbohydrate as regular jam.

Food Choices	Large Meal	Small Meal
Carbohydrate	$3\frac{1}{2}$	2
Meat and Alternatives	$\frac{1}{2}$	$\frac{1}{2}$
Nutritional Info	Large Meal	Small Meal
Carbohydrate	57 g	36 g
Fiber	7 g	5 g

Your Breakfast Menu	Large Meal (370 calories)	Small Meal (250 calories)
Brown toast	2 slices	1 slice
Peanut butter	1 tbsp (15 mL)	1 tbsp (15 mL)
Jam or jelly	1 tsp (5 mL) regular jam, or 2 tsp (10 mL) diet jam	–
Skim or 1% milk	$\frac{1}{2}$ cup (125 mL)	$\frac{1}{2}$ cup (125 mL)
Apple slices	$\frac{1}{2}$ medium apple	$\frac{1}{2}$ medium apple

SMALL MEAL

BREAKFAST 5

Hot Cereal

Hot cereals such as porridge (oatmeal), oat bran, whole grain cereals and corn meal cereal are high in fiber. Adding 1 tablespoon (15 mL) of wheat bran to your hot cereal will give you even more fiber. If you add 1 to 2 teaspoons (5 to 10 mL) of ground flaxseed to your cereal, you will have a source of omega-3 fats.

If you don't add any sugar to your cereal, or if you use a low-calorie sweetener, you may have a whole fruit serving (as shown with most of the other breakfasts).

Packaged single servings of oatmeal are fast and easy, but most have a lot of sugar added. Look for the ones that say "plain" or "natural" and check that sugar is not listed in the ingredients.

You may want to mix half a package of instant unsweetened oatmeal with half a package of one of the flavored oatmeals. This way you'll get a lightly sweetened oatmeal and you can add a half fruit serving.

Have a full fruit serving of fruit if you don't choose sugar:
- *2 tablespoons (25 mL) of raisins*
- *2 prunes or dried apricots*
- *1/4 cup (60 mL) prune juice.*

Research shows that people who eat breakfast find it easier to lose weight and keep it off and are more likely to get all the nutrients the body needs to be healthy.

Food Choices	Large Meal	Small Meal
Carbohydrate	4½	3

Nutritional Info	Large Meal	Small Meal
Carbohydrate	73 g	47 g
Fiber	6 g	4 g

Your Breakfast Menu	Large Meal (370 calories)	Small Meal (250 calories)
Hot cereal	1½ cups (375 mL) cooked (9 tbsp/135 mL dry)	1 cup (250 mL) cooked (6 tbsp/90 mL dry)
Brown sugar	2 tsp (10 mL)	2 tsp (10 mL)
Raisins	2 tbsp (25 mL)	1 tbsp (15 mL)
Skim or 1% milk	1 cup (250 mL)	½ cup (125 mL)

SMALL MEAL

French Toast

French toast is quick and easy to make.

This breakfast is served with fruit and syrup. If you don't have fresh strawberries, any other kind of fruit, either fresh, frozen or canned in juice, will do.

Two tablespoons (25 mL) of light syrup or 2 teaspoons (10 mL) of diet jam are the same as 1 tablespoon (15 mL) of regular syrup.

French Toast

Makes 4 pieces of toast

2 large eggs	
¼ cup (50 mL) skim milk	
Pinch salt, if desired	
4 slices bread	

Ground nutmeg or cinnamon (optional)

Per piece	
Calories	110
Carbohydrate	14 g
Fiber	1 g
Protein	6 g
Fat, total	3 g
Fat, saturated	1 g
Cholesterol	93 mg
Sodium	191 mg

1. In a medium bowl, beat the eggs with a fork or whisk. Add the milk and salt.
2. Dip the bread into the egg and milk.
3. At medium heat, in a nonstick pan, cook both sides until golden brown. See page 50 if you don't have a nonstick pan.
4. Sprinkle with nutmeg or cinnamon, if desired.

Variation: Add 2 tsp (10 mL) grated orange zest to the egg mixture for a nice orange flavor.

Bread slices vary from brand to brand. This recipe is based on bread with 60 to 70 calories per 30-gram slice. If your slices are larger, keep your serving to two slices for the large meal and one slice for the small meal.

Food Choices	Large Meal	Small Meal
Carbohydrate	4	2½
Meat and Alternatives	1½	1
Nutritional Info	**Large Meal**	**Small Meal**
Carbohydrate	61 g	41 g
Fiber	4 g	3 g

Your Breakfast Menu	Large Meal (370 calories)	Small Meal (250 calories)
French Toast	3 slices	2 slices
Jam	1 tbsp (15 mL), or 2 tbsp (25 mL) diet jam	2 tsp (10 mL), or 4 tsp (20 mL) diet jam
Strawberries	5 medium	4 medium

SMALL MEAL

BREAKFAST 7

Muffin & Yogurt

Large bought muffins can have as much as 3 to 5 teaspoons (15 to 25 mL) of hidden fat. Try making these delicious, low-fat muffins. They only have ½ teaspoon (2 mL) of added fat in each muffin.

Instead of yogurt, have 1 cup (250 mL) of low-fat milk. For the small meal, you could have a slice of low-fat cheese instead of yogurt. See page 90, Lunch 7, to learn more about choosing yogurt.

Bran Muffins

Makes 12 medium muffins

1 cup (250 mL) flour	**Per muffin**
1½ tsp (7 mL) baking powder	Calories............144
½ tsp (2 mL) baking soda	Carbohydrate.....29 g
	Fiber...............4 g
½ tsp (2 mL) salt	Protein............4 g
¼ cup (50 mL) unsweetened applesauce	Fat, total..........3 g
2 tbsp (25 mL) margarine or vegetable oil	Fat, saturated......0 g
	Cholesterol.....16 mg
¼ cup (50 mL) packed brown sugar	Sodium.......234 mg

1 cup (250 mL) flour
1½ tsp (7 mL) baking powder
½ tsp (2 mL) baking soda
½ tsp (2 mL) salt
¼ cup (50 mL) unsweetened applesauce
2 tbsp (25 mL) margarine or vegetable oil
¼ cup (50 mL) packed brown sugar
¼ cup (50 mL) molasses (or honey)
1 egg
1 cup (250 mL) skim milk
1½ cups (375 mL) wheat bran
½ cup (125 mL) raisins

Per muffin
Calories............144
Carbohydrate.....29 g
Fiber...............4 g
Protein............4 g
Fat, total..........3 g
Fat, saturated......0 g
Cholesterol.....16 mg
Sodium.......234 mg

1. In a medium bowl, mix flour, baking powder, soda and salt together.
2. In a large bowl, combine applesauce, margarine and brown sugar. Stir with a wooden spoon until well mixed.
3. Beat in the molasses and the egg. Add the milk, then add the wheat bran.
4. Add the flour mixture to the large bowl. Then add the raisins. The mixture will be wet.
5. Spoon into an ungreased nonstick muffin tin. If you don't have a nonstick tin, use paper cups or lightly grease your muffin tin. Bake in a 400°F (200°C) oven for 20 to 25 minutes. They are ready when a toothpick put into the center of a muffin comes out clean.

Food Choices	Large Meal	Small Meal
Carbohydrate	3½	3½
Meat and Alternatives	1	–
Fat	½	½
Nutritional Info	**Large Meal**	**Small Meal**
Carbohydrate	51 g	51 g
Fiber	5 g	5 g

Your Breakfast Menu	Large Meal (370 calories)	Small Meal (250 calories)
Bran Muffin	1	1
Low-fat fruit yogurt with low-calorie sweetener	¾ cup (175 mL)	¾ cup (175 mL)
Orange	½ medium	½ medium
Piece of cheese	1 oz (30 g)	–

SMALL MEAL

BREAKFAST 8

Raisin Toast & Cheese

Raisin toast makes a nice change, but remember that slice for slice it contains more carbohydrate than whole-grain toast. You may want to have half your toast with the cheese broiled on top. The rest of the toast can be served with a thin spread of jam, which has fewer calories than margarine.

The large meal can include either 1 ounce (30 g) of brick cheese or 1½ slices of cheese. If you choose low-fat cheese, you will get less fat. Check the label:
- A low-fat block cheese or cheese slice has 20% or less milk fat (20% M.F.).
- Regular-fat cheese has about 35% milk fat.

Enjoy half a grapefruit or choose one serving of another type of fruit, such as:
- 1 medium apple
- 1 peach
- 1 small banana
- 1 orange

Grapefruit treat:
A nice way to have grapefruit is to sprinkle it with a bit of cinnamon and low-calorie sweetener. Then, microwave it for thirty seconds or broil it until warm.

> When you eat breakfast, even the small one, you will wake up your body and have more energy. Eating breakfast will help you control your blood sugar.

Instead of 2 slices of raisin toast, you could have 1 raisin scone or 1 hot cross bun.

Instead of the cheese shown, you may choose 1 cup (250 mL) of milk.

Food Choices	Large Meal	Small Meal
Carbohydrate	4	2½
Meat and Alternatives	1	½
Nutritional Info	**Large Meal**	**Small Meal**
Carbohydrate	57 g	38 g
Fiber	6 g	4 g

Your Breakfast Menu	Large Meal (370 calories)	Small Meal (250 calories)
Raisin toast	3 slices	2 slices
Jam or jelly	1 tsp (5 mL), or 2 tsp (10 mL) diet jam	– –
Cheese slice	1½ slices (1 oz/30 g)	1 slice (⅔ oz/20 g)
Grapefruit	½ small	½ small

SMALL MEAL

BREAKFAST 9

Waffle & Hot Cocoa

Store-bought frozen waffles make an easy, quick breakfast. The plain waffles have fewer calories. For a treat, you may want to choose waffles that have blueberries or other fruits added.

Have your waffle with a small amount of jam, honey or syrup, as shown in the box below.

There is one fruit serving included with this breakfast.

Light hot cocoa mixes come in a variety of flavors. They are made with skim milk powder and are sweetened with a low-calorie sweetener. Choose a light hot cocoa mix that has fewer than 50 calories in a ³⁄₄-cup (175 mL) serving. Check the label.

You can make this homemade hot chocolate for a change from the packaged mixes. One cupful (250 mL) contains a cup of milk.

Choose one of these instead of 1 cup (250 mL) of light hot cocoa:
- *1 cup (250 mL) low-fat milk*
- *³⁄₄ cup (175 mL) low-fat yogurt*

Food Choices	Large Meal	Small Meal
Carbohydrate	4½	3½
Fat	1	½
Nutritional Info	**Large Meal**	**Small Meal**
Carbohydrate	65 g	51 g
Fiber	3 g	2 g

Homemade Hot Chocolate

Makes 1 cup (250 mL)

1 cup (250 mL) skim milk

1 tsp (5 mL) cocoa

¼ tsp (1 mL) instant decaffeinated coffee (optional)

1 tsp (5 mL) sugar or low-calorie sweetener of your choice

Cinnamon stick or a pinch of ground cinnamon

Per serving	
Calories	106
Carbohydrate	17 g
Fiber	1 g
Protein	9 g
Fat, total	1 g
Fat, saturated	0 g
Cholesterol	4 mg
Sodium	127 mg

1. Whisk ingredients in a microwavable jar or a glass measuring cup.
2. Microwave for 2 to 3 minutes, whisking at least once, until boiling.

Your Breakfast Menu	Large Meal (370 calories)	Small Meal (250 calories)
Waffles	2	1
Margarine or butter	1 tsp (5 mL)	½ tsp (2 mL) margarine
Syrup (or, honey or jam)	1 tbsp (15 mL), or 2 tbsp (25 mL) light syrup	1 tbsp (15 mL), or 2 tbsp (25 mL) light syrup
Grapes	15	15
Light hot chocolate	1 cup (250 mL) (½ oz/14 g package) made with water	1 cup (250 mL) (½ oz/14 g package) made with water

SMALL MEAL

Protein Smoothie & Fruit Bar

Benefits of soy

Tofu is processed from soybeans, which have protein without the fat and cholesterol. Soybeans contain natural compounds called isoflavones. These compounds may help reduce the bad LDL cholesterol and increase the good HDL cholesterol. For men, isoflavones may also help to protect against enlargement of the prostate. For women, they may help to reduce the risk for breast cancer and may help relieve some of the symptoms of menopause. Check that the tofu is fortified with calcium.

If you're expecting a long morning ahead, without a chance for a snack, it's smart to eat protein for breakfast so you won't feel hungry by mid-morning. Here are two protein breakfast smoothies you can try.

Instead of a fruit bar or granola bar, you could have a Bran Muffin from Breakfast 7.

Soy Fruit Smoothie

Makes 2 cups (500 mL)

5¼ oz (150 g) flavored dessert tofu (such as peach, mango, berry or lime)

¼ cup (50 mL) non-fat peach- or vanilla-flavored yogurt (no sugar added)

½ cup (125 mL) skim milk

2 peach halves (fresh or canned, juice-packed) or ½ small banana

Per 1 cup (250 mL)	
Calories	108
Carbohydrate	18 g
Fiber	1 g
Protein	6 g
Fat, total	1 g
Fat, saturated	0 g
Cholesterol	2 mg
Sodium	72 mg

1. Place all ingredients in a blender and blend until smooth.

Yogurt Fruit Smoothie

Makes 2 cups (500 mL)

¾ cup (175 mL) non-fat peach-flavored yogurt (no sugar added)

½ cup (125 mL) skim milk

3 tbsp (45 mL) skim milk powder

2 peach halves (fresh or canned, juice-packed) or ½ small banana

1 tsp (5 mL) honey

Small pinch cinnamon (optional)

Per 1 cup (250 mL)	
Calories	118
Carbohydrate	21 g
Fiber	1 g
Protein	8 g
Fat, total	0 g
Fat, saturated	0 g
Cholesterol	4 mg
Sodium	123 mg

1. Place all ingredients in a blender and blend until smooth.

Food Choices	Large Meal	Small Meal
Carbohydrate	4	3
Meat and Alternatives	1	½
Nutritional Info	**Large Meal**	**Small Meal**
Carbohydrate	69 g	51 g
Fiber	5 g	4 g

Your Breakfast Menu	Large Meal (370 calories)	Small Meal (250 calories)
Soy Fruit Smoothie (or Yogurt Fruit Smoothie)	2 cups (500 mL)	1 cup (250 mL)
Fruit bar or granola bar	1 (less than 150 calories)	1 (less than 150 calories)

SMALL MEAL

Fiesta Breakfast

Beans and rice are commonly served for breakfast throughout Latin America. I tried this breakfast for the first time while traveling in Brazil, where it was served with the classic Café Americano (hot milk and coffee). To relive the adventure, I offer this recipe, with the spicy flavors of onion and garlic, to give you a spirited start to your day. The recipe can be made ahead and reheated. Serve with a scrambled egg cooked in a nonstick pan, salsa and cucumbers.

Mexican Rice and Beans

Makes just over 2 cups (500 mL)

Per 1 cup (250 mL)	
Calories	261
Carbohydrate	45 g
Fiber	7 g
Protein	9 g
Fat, total	5 g
Fat, saturated	1 g
Cholesterol	0 mg
Sodium	272 mg

2 tsp (10 mL) olive oil or vegetable oil

1 small or ½ medium onion, finely chopped

3 cloves garlic, minced

½ tsp (2 mL) ground cumin

½ tsp (2 mL) dried oregano

1 tbsp (15 mL) chopped fresh cilantro or parsley

¼ tsp (1 mL) hot pepper flakes (optional)

1 cup (250 mL) canned black beans (½ of a 19-oz/540 mL can)

1 cup (250 mL) cooked rice

1. To a frying pan, add the oil, onions, garlic, cumin, oregano, cilantro and hot pepper flakes, if using. Cook, stirring, over medium heat until the onions are soft.
2. While the onions are cooking, empty the beans into a sieve, rinse them with cold water and drain.
3. Stir the cooked rice and rinsed beans into the pan with the cooked onions. Place in a covered casserole dish in a warm oven while you scramble the eggs. Or refrigerate, to reheat the next morning.

Café Americano

Makes 1 cup (250 mL)

Per 1 cup (250 mL)	
Calories	88
Carbohydrate	12 g
Fiber	0 g
Protein	8 g
Fat, total	0 g
Fat, saturated	0 g
Cholesterol	4 mg
Sodium	127 mg

1 cup (250 mL) skim milk

1 tsp (5 mL) instant coffee

Sweetener, to taste

1. Heat milk in microwave until boiling, for about 2 to 3 minutes, then add instant coffee and low-calorie sweetener. (If you use regular sugar, limit to 1 tsp/5 mL.)

Food Choices	Large Meal	Small Meal
Carbohydrate	3	2
Meat and Alternatives	2	1½
Fat	1	½
Nutritional Info	**Large Meal**	**Small Meal**
Carbohydrate	49 g	30 g
Fiber	6 g	3 g

Your Breakfast Menu	Large Meal (370 calories)	Small Meal (250 calories)
Mexican Rice and Beans	¾ cup (175 mL)	⅓ cup (75 mL)
Scrambled egg	1 large	1 large
Salsa	2 tbsp (25 mL)	2 tbsp (25 mL)
Sliced cucumbers	6 slices	6 slices
Café Americano	1 cup (250 mL)	1 cup (250 mL)

Fast-Food Breakfast

If you are tempted to eat breakfast at a fast-food restaurant or coffee shop, then carefully choose your meal. Portion sizes are often large or extra-large, and loaded with fat, sugar, salt and calories. Ask for their nutrient guides, or visit their websites. Then you can check which items would fit into your large-meal breakfast of 370 calories or your small-meal breakfast of 250 calories.

How calories add up:

Beverages: Large-size specialty cappuccinos have 500 calories or more. Juices come in large containers, so are high in calories from sugar ("natural" sugar, and in some cases extra added sugar).

Muffins and donuts: Muffins have become so large that they are exploding with calories. Typically, a donut has 200 to 400 calories, while a fast-food muffin has 300 to 500 calories! Your lowest-calorie choice may be the old-fashioned cake donut, at about 200 calories, rather than a muffin.

Bagels: One large bagel is equal to 4 slices of regular bread, or 300 calories. A large buttered bagel has 400 to 500 calories, and if you add cream cheese it goes up to 500 to 650 calories.

Tea biscuits: A tea biscuit can have 150 to 300 calories, depending on its size. If you add margarine or butter, you add 45 calories for each teaspoon. Complete-meal tea biscuits that include bacon, egg and cheese or fruits and sugar can have 400 to 500 calories.

English muffins: A plain egg English muffin has about 300 calories, but if you choose one with added sausage and cheese, your calories will be 500 or more.

Croissant: A standard-size croissant has 200 to 300 calories, but if you eat a double-croissant sandwich with sausage, egg and cheese, expect 500 calories.

Burritos: A plain breakfast burrito has about 400 calories; a super-sized breakfast burrito has 600 to 800 calories.

Alternative menu choices you could have for the same calories:

Large meal
*Plain bagel, unbuttered, + $1/2$ serving of light cream cheese **or** 1 low-fat blueberry muffin **or** 1 cake donut. 1 cup (250 mL) coffee or tea with single milk, low-calorie sweetener if desired.*

Small meal
*1 croissant or cake donut **or** a bowl of soup **or** a single cookie, such as apple cinnamon. 1 cup (250 mL) coffee or tea with single milk, low-calorie sweetener if desired.*

Your Breakfast Menu	Large Meal (370 calories)	Small Meal (250 calories)
Option #1 Entrée	1-egg English muffin or cheeseburger	1 English muffin + single jam or fruit/yogurt parfait or chicken fajita
Apple juice Coffee or tea with single milk, low-calorie sweetener	6¾ oz (177 mL) 1 cup (250 mL)	6¾ oz (177 mL) 1 cup (250 mL)

SMALL MEAL

BREAKFAST 13

Granola Combo

This combo of fruit, yogurt and protein-rich granola can be enjoyed at home or carried with you to work.

This homemade granola is intensely nutritious because it is rich in protein and healthy fats from the sunflower seeds and nuts. If you want to substitute a store-bought granola or cereal, measure a portion equal to 150 calories for the large meal or 110 calories for the small meal. Look for a cereal that is low in saturated fat, trans fat and sugar. Keep in mind that a store-bought cereal may not give you the same protein boost that is found in this Crunchy Nut Granola.

Crunchy Nut Granola

Makes 10 cups (2.5 L).

½ cup (125 mL) shelled sunflower seeds

¾ cup (175 mL) sweetened flaked coconut

¼ cup (50 mL) wheat germ

¼ cup (50 mL) ground flaxseed

1 cup (250 mL) chopped or sliced almonds, walnuts or pecans

4 cups (1 L) large-flake old-fashioned rolled oats

½ cup (125 mL) corn syrup

2 tbsp (25 mL) olive oil or vegetable oil

1 tsp (5 mL) vanilla

1 tsp (5 mL) almond extract or coconut extract

2 cups (500 mL) crisp rice or round oat cereal

½ cup (125 mL) raisins or other dried fruit, chopped

Per 1 cup (250 mL)	
Calories	429
Carbohydrate	58 g
Fiber	8 g
Protein	11 g
Fat, total	19 g
Fat, saturated	4 g
Cholesterol	0 mg
Sodium	104 mg

1. In a large bowl, mix the sunflower seeds, coconut, wheat germ, ground flaxseed, nuts and oats.
2. In a small bowl, combine corn syrup, oil, vanilla and almond or coconut extract.
3. Add the syrup mixture to the dry ingredients. Make sure any wet lumps are well blended in.
4. Place granola in a large casserole dish and bake on middle rack at 350°F (180°C) for 30 to 35 minutes, or until slightly toasted. During baking, remove the pan from the oven *every 10 minutes* and stir, so that the granola cooks evenly.
5. Once toasted, remove from the oven and *right away* transfer to a metal bowl or pot; otherwise, the granola may stick to the bottom of the hot pan as it sits to cool. Stir once or twice as it's cooling. Once cooled, add cereal and raisins. Store in an airtight container.

Food Choices	Large Meal	Small Meal
Carbohydrate	3½	2½
Fat	2	1
Nutritional Info	**Large Meal**	**Small Meal**
Carbohydrate	63 g	42 g
Fiber	9 g	5 g

Your Breakfast Menu	Large Meal (370 calories)	Small Meal (250 calories)
Chopped fruit (fresh, frozen or canned)	1½ cups (375 mL)	1 cup (250 mL)
Fruit-flavored yogurt, low-fat, low-sugar	¾ cup (175 mL)	¾ cup (175 mL)
Crunchy Nut Granola	½ cup (125 mL)	¼ cup (60 mL)
Tea or coffee	1 cup (250 mL)	1 cup (250 mL)

BREAKFAST 14

Prairie Quiche

The Prairies and Great Plains grow a large amount of the world's wheat, which is ground into the flour that we bake into bread. Prairie Quiche has a bread crumb crust, which is much lower in calories and fat than a traditional pastry crust. The quiche takes about 45 minutes to prepare and cook, so it's perfect when you have a carefree morning ahead. This recipe is delicious and satisfying, but because it's high in fat it should be an occasional treat.

Four- or 5-blend shredded cheese
Where shredded cheese is an ingredient in recipes, you can use a 4- or 5-blend, which may include cheddar, mozzarella, parmesan and specialty cheeses.

Prairie Quiche

Makes 2 large or 3 small servings

½ tsp (2 mL) margarine or butter, to grease the casserole

⅓ cup (75 mL) dry bread crumbs

2 eggs

2 slices raw bacon, fat partly trimmed off, chopped, or 2 slices turkey bacon

½ cup (125 mL) skim milk

Pinch of black pepper

¾ cup (175 mL) sweet red pepper or broccoli (or a combination), chopped into small pieces

½ cup (125 mL) light shredded cheese

Per ½ quiche	
Calories	310
Carbohydrate	21 g
Fiber	2 g
Protein	20 g
Fat, total	16 g
Fat, saturated	7 g
Cholesterol	214 mg
Sodium	615 mg

1. Grease the sides and bottom of a 6-inch (15 cm) casserole dish with margarine or butter. Spread the bread crumbs on the bottom of the casserole dish.
2. In a bowl, combine eggs, chopped bacon, milk, pepper and vegetables. Pour on top of the bread crumbs. Top with the shredded cheese.
3. Bake in oven on the middle rack at 400°F (200°C) for 25 minutes.
4. Once cooked, remove from the oven and let sit for 5 minutes. Gently remove slices with an egg turner.

A small glass of orange, apple, grapefruit or cranberry juice is served with the Prairie Quiche. Juice is an excellent source of vitamin C, but is a high source of natural sugar and lacks the fiber found in fresh fruit. It can be chosen for an occasional breakfast choice instead of a fresh fruit. (See page 13.)

Food Choices	Large Meal	Small Meal
Carbohydrate	2	2
Meat and Alternatives	2	1
Fat	1	1
Nutritional Info	**Large Meal**	**Small Meal**
Carbohydrate	33 g	26 g
Fiber	2 g	1 g

Your Breakfast Menu	Large Meal (370 calories)	Small Meal (250 calories)
Quiche Orange juice, unsweetened	½ of the recipe ½ cup (125 mL)	⅓ of the recipe ½ cup (125 mL)

SMALL MEAL

BREAKFAST 15

Irish Currant Cake

This yummy cake is a sweet adaptation of traditional Irish soda bread, and is definitely worth trying. The recipe uses currants, which are dried from a small seedless variety of grape (you can replace the currants with raisins).

When you cook with a cast-iron pan or pot, your food becomes enriched with the iron.

Papaya is a tropical fruit rich in potassium and vitamins A and C. An alternative would be a similar portion of cantaloupe.

Irish Currant Cake

Makes 10 slices

Per slice	
Calories	209
Carbohydrate	38 g
Fiber	2 g
Protein	4 g
Fat, total	4 g
Fat, saturated	2 g
Cholesterol	29 mg
Sodium	259 mg

2 cups (500 mL) flour

½ tsp (2 mL) salt

1½ tsp (7 mL) baking powder

½ tsp (2 mL) baking soda

½ cup (125 mL) sugar

¾ cup (175 mL) dried currants

1 egg

1 cup (250 mL) buttermilk (if you don't have buttermilk, start with 2 tbsp/25 mL vinegar and add skim or 1% milk to make up 1 cup/250 mL)

3 tbsp (45 mL) butter, melted

1. In a bowl, mix together the flour, salt, baking powder, baking soda and sugar. Sift out any lumps.
2. Add the currants to the dry ingredients and toss until they are well coated in flour.
3. Beat the egg with a fork in a small bowl. Add the buttermilk and the melted butter to the egg and stir with the fork.
4. Add this milk mixture to the dry ingredients and blend until all the flour is mixed in.
5. Turn the batter into a greased 10-inch (25 cm) cast-iron pan, a 9- by 5-inch (2 L) loaf pan or a 7½-inch (18 cm) square baking pan. Or drop as 12 biscuits onto a greased cookie sheet.
6. Bake at 350°F (180°C) for 30 to 40 minutes, until golden brown. Cool slightly. If baked in a pan, turn the pan upside down onto a plate and the cake will fall out. Let it sit for a few minutes, then turn it over again and slice it, serving it still warm.

Food Choices	Large Meal	Small Meal
Carbohydrate	4	3
Fat	2	1
Nutritional Info	Large Meal	Small Meal
Carbohydrate	56 g	52 g
Fiber	3 g	3 g

Your Breakfast Menu	Large Meal (370 calories)	Small Meal (250 calories)
Irish Currant Cake	1 slice	1 slice
Margarine	1 tsp (5 mL)	—
Jam or marmalade	1 tbsp (15 mL) regular	1 tsp (5 mL) regular or 2 tsp (10 mL) light
Papaya with lime juice	½ small	½ small
Tea or coffee	1 cup (250 mL)	1 cup (250 mL)

SMALL MEAL

Lunch Meals

- **each large lunch has 520 calories**
- **each small lunch has 400 calories**

LUNCH 1

Sandwich with Milk

There are many nutritious fillings for sandwiches; for example, roast beef (as shown in the photograph), chicken or turkey breast, lean meat, cheese, egg or fish. For a lower-salt option, choose home-cooked meat instead of deli meats. Tuna, salmon or sardine sandwiches are also great choices; see Lunch 12, Tuna Sandwich.

Each sandwich shown is made with 2 teaspoons (10 mL) of light mayonnaise. You may choose to use no fat at all, or use only 1 teaspoon (5 mL) of relish or mustard, or 1 tablespoon (15 mL) of salsa, which are all low in fat.

If you want a chopped filling, you can add celery, onion, green pepper or any other vegetable, with just a little light mayonnaise. Add your mayonnaise to the filling instead of on your bread.

Include some kind of vegetable on the side, such as three radishes, a stalk of celery, or a few slices of tomato or green pepper.

Cantaloupe or any other type of fruit serving is good with this meal.

You can have 1 cup (250 mL) of skim milk, 1% milk or buttermilk, or ¾ cup (175 mL) of light yogurt. If you would like a slice of cheese as an extra in your sandwich, don't have the milk to drink.

Food Choices	Large Meal	Small Meal
Carbohydrate	5	4
Meat and Alternatives	2	1
Fat	1	1
Nutritional Info	Large Meal	Small Meal
Carbohydrate	76 g	61 g
Fiber	7 g	5 g

Your Lunch Menu	Large Meal (520 calories)	Small Meal (400 calories)
Meat sandwich	1½ sandwiches	1 sandwich
• bread, light rye	• 3 slices	• 2 slices
• roast beef	• 2 oz (60 g)	• 1 oz (30 g)
• light mayonnaise	• 1 tbsp (15 mL)	• 1 tbsp (15 mL)
• lettuce	• 2 large leaves	• 2 large leaves
Radishes	3	3
Cantaloupe	½ small (1½ cups/375 mL diced)	½ small (1½ cups/375 mL diced)
Skim or 1% milk	1 cup (250 mL)	1 cup (250 mL)

SMALL MEAL

LUNCH 2

Beans & Toast

Open a can of brown beans, warm them up and serve a portion of them, as shown, with toast and fresh vegetables. Remove any chunks of pork fat from the baked beans, or buy beans canned only in tomato sauce.

For a change from toast, eat your beans with bannock (see page 133 for recipe) or another type of bread.

If you don't have any celery, choose a sliced tomato or $1/2$ cup (125 mL) of tomato or vegetable juice.

Look for ice cream bars that are marked light or low-fat, and that are sweetened with a low-calorie sweetener. They taste good and have calcium. If you want to make your own low-fat and low-sugar frozen treats, try these Frozen Yogurt Bars.

For a change, choose canned spaghetti instead of beans.

Check the labels of light ice cream bars. Choose the ones that have fewer than 50 calories. One regular ice cream bar will have at least 150 calories.

Instead of a light ice cream bar or home-made Frozen Yogurt Bar, you could have $1/2$ cup (125 mL) of milk.

Frozen Yogurt Bars

Makes 8 bars

2 cups (500 mL) plain skim milk yogurt

$1/2$ tsp (5 mL) diet (sugar-free) fruit flavored drink crystals

1. Mix the crystals with the yogurt.
2. Pour into containers and freeze.

Ready to eat in 2 to 3 hours.

Per bar	
Calories	32
Carbohydrate	5 g
Fiber	0 g
Protein	3 g
Fat, total	0 g
Fat, saturated	0 g
Cholesterol	1 mg
Sodium	46 mg

Food Choices	Large Meal	Small Meal
Carbohydrate	4	3
Meat and Alternatives	2	1
Fat	2	2
Nutritional Info	**Large Meal**	**Small Meal**
Carbohydrate	86 g	59 g
Fiber	15 g	10 g

Your Lunch Menu	Large Meal (520 calories)	Small Meal (400 calories)
Canned baked beans	1 cup (250 mL)	$1/2$ cup (125 mL)
Toast	$1^1/2$ slices	$1^1/2$ slices
Margarine	2 tsp (10 mL)	2 tsp (10 mL)
Celery sticks	2 stalks	2 stalks
Frozen Yogurt Bar	1	1

SMALL MEAL

Good

Chicken Soup & Bagel

Canned soup or packaged soups are quick and easy. Add a handful of frozen vegetables for added nutrition. Cream soups have extra fat, so choose them less often. Try this recipe.

Instead of both salmon and cream cheese, a bagel could be served with any of these:

- *1 ounce (30 g) or one thin slice of cheese or meat such as ham or turkey. Limit high-fat meats like bologna and salami.*
- *¼ cup (60 mL) canned fish*
- *2 tablespoons (25 mL) peanut butter*

Chicken Rice Soup

Makes 7½ cups (1.875 mL)

2 medium carrots, chopped

1 medium onion, chopped

2 stalks celery, chopped

¼ cup (50 mL) rice (uncooked)

1 package (2 oz/60 g) of dried chicken noodle soup mix

½ tsp (2 mL) of dried dill

6 cups (1.5 L) of water

1. Chop carrots, onion and celery.
2. Put all ingredients in a medium pot.
3. Cover and gently boil for about 20 minutes, until the carrots are cooked. Stir occasionally.

Per 1 cup (250 mL)	
Calories	67
Carbohydrate	13 g
Fiber	1 g
Protein	2 g
Fat, total	1 g
Fat, saturated	0 g
Cholesterol	6 mg
Sodium	316 mg

It is important to note that the bagel in this meal is a 3-inch (7.5 cm) bagel weighing 2 ounces (60 g), and it equals 2 slices of bread. Larger bagels can equal 5 or more slices of bread.

The bagel is served with light cream cheese, and salmon, tomato and onion. For a change, try smoked salmon (lox).

Food Choices	Large Meal	Small Meal
Carbohydrate	4½	3
Meat and Alternatives	1	1
Fat	1	½
Nutritional Info	**Large Meal**	**Small Meal**
Carbohydrate	76 g	60 g
Fiber	7 g	6 g

Your Lunch Menu	Large Meal (520 calories)	Small Meal (400 calories)
Chicken Rice Soup	1½ cups (375 mL)	1½ cups (375 mL)
Soda crackers	2	2
Bagel	1 (or 2 slices bread)	½ (or 1 slice bread)
Light cream cheese (20% fat)	2 tbsp (25 mL)	1 tbsp (15 mL)
Canned pink or red salmon	¼ cup (60 mL)	¼ cup (60 mL)
Tomato	½ medium	½ medium
Sliced onion	2 slices	2 slices
Orange	1 medium	1 medium

SMALL MEAL

Macaroni & Cheese

Boxed macaroni and cheese is an easy choice for lunch. Prepare according to package directions, adding milk, the powdered cheese and just 1 tbsp (15 mL) of margarine.

For extra calcium, you can mix in 2 tablespoons (25 mL) of skim milk powder with the macaroni and cheese.

If you would prefer a homemade macaroni and cheese, there is a recipe with Dinner 18.

Green or yellow beans can be fresh, frozen or canned. Steam or microwave vegetables, or very lightly boil them. Overcooked vegetables lose important vitamins and minerals as well as good flavor.

A few olives or a slice of avocado are a good source of healthy monounsaturated fat.

If you don't have any green or yellow beans, choose raw vegetables such as:
- *up to 3 celery stalks*
- *1 medium carrot*
- *1 large tomato*
- *1/2 medium cucumber*

Usually 1/2 cup (125 mL) of cooked macaroni is 1 Carbohydrate choice. However, the smaller and more compact noodles in the boxed macaroni and cheese fit closer together. So 1/3 cup (75 mL) is 1 Carbohydrate choice.

If you would like a slice of bread with this lunch, cut the macaroni and cheese by 1/3 cup (75 mL).

Food Choices	Large Meal	Small Meal
Carbohydrate	5	4
Fat	1	1/2
Nutritional Info	Large Meal	Small Meal
Carbohydrate	99 g	83 g
Fiber	8 g	7 g

Your Lunch Menu	Large Meal (520 calories)	Small Meal (400 calories)
Macaroni & Cheese	1 1/3 cups (325 mL)	1 cup (250 mL)
Green beans	1 cup (250 mL)	1 cup (250 mL)
Green olives	3	1
Apple	1 medium	1 medium

SMALL MEAL

Toasted Cheese & Tomato Sandwich

Coleslaw from a restaurant or store-bought has a lot of fat in the dressing. Try this low-fat recipe.

Mayonnaise has about the same calories as margarine or butter. Light mayonnaise or calorie-reduced margarine has one-third the calories or less. These light brands have fewer than 45 calories in 1 tablespoon (15 mL).

Coleslaw

Makes 6½ cups (1.625 mL)

4 cups (1 L) shredded cabbage

4 medium carrots, grated

4 stalks celery, finely chopped

1 small onion or 2 green onions

3 tbsp (45 mL) light mayonnaise

1 tbsp (15 mL) sugar

¼ cup (50 mL) vinegar

¼ tsp (1 mL) garlic powder

Salt and pepper, to taste

Per ½ cup (125 mL)
Calories 33
Carbohydrate . . . . . . 5 g
Fiber. . . . . 1 g
Protein . . . . 1 g
Fat, total . . . . 1 g
Fat, saturated . . . . . . 0 g
Cholesterol . . . . . . 1 mg
Sodium. . . . . 47 mg

1. Chop the cabbage in fine strips, grate the carrots, and finely chop the celery and onion. Mix these together in a large bowl.
2. In a small bowl, mix the mayonnaise, sugar, vinegar, garlic powder, salt and pepper. Add to the cabbage. Mix well.
3. Cover and put in the fridge. This will keep well for 1 week.

Food Choices	Large Meal	Small Meal
Carbohydrate	4½	3½
Meat and Alternatives	1	½
Fat	½	½
Nutritional Info	**Large Meal**	**Small Meal**
Carbohydrate	79 g	59 g
Fiber	11 g	8 g

Your Lunch Menu	Large Meal (520 calories)	Small Meal (400 calories)
Toasted cheese & tomato sandwich	1½ sandwiches	1 sandwich
• bread	• 3 slices	• 2 slices
• cheese	• 1½ slices	• 1 slice
• tomato	• 1 large	• 1 medium
• lettuce	• 1 to 2 leaves	• 1 to 2 leaves
• light mayonnaise	• 2 tsp (10 mL)	• 2 tsp (10 mL)
Coleslaw (or raw veggies)	½ cup (125 mL)	½ cup (125 mL)
Cherries	½ cup (125 mL)	½ cup (125 mL)
Skim or 1% milk	½ cup (125 mL)	½ cup (125 mL)

SMALL MEAL

LUNCH 6

Cold Plate with Soup

The vegetable soup may be dried or canned. Dried soups usually have fewer calories than canned.

For a lower-salt option, make a soup with homemade salt-free chicken or beef broth. Add your favorite vegetables, herbs and pepper.

Soda crackers are very low in fat. They have little fat compared with snack crackers. Choose the unsalted soda crackers.

Instead of the small bun shown, you could have a slice of bread, half an English muffin, 1 small bran muffin, 4 melba toasts or 7 soda crackers.

If you don't usually eat cottage cheese, have a slice of low-fat hard cheese instead.

You may choose 14 hot pepper rings (pickled) instead of a dill pickle. Or, for a less salty choice, choose sliced cucumber in vinegar.

Have a fruit serving with your cold plate, either fresh, frozen or canned (in water or juice).

*S*hop for low-fat cheese:
- *1% cottage cheese*
- *block cheese that is 20% M.F. (milk fat) or less*

Food Choices	Large Meal	Small Meal
Carbohydrate	3½	3½
Meat and Alternatives	4	2
Nutritional Info	**Large Meal**	**Small Meal**
Carbohydrate	74 g	71 g
Fiber	9 g	9 g

Your Lunch Menu	Large Meal (520 calories)	Small Meal (400 calories)
Vegetable soup (packaged) Cold plate	1 cup (250 mL)	1 cup (250 mL)
• 1% cottage cheese	1 cup (250 mL)	½ cup (125 mL)
• peaches	2 halves	2 halves
• dill pickle	1 medium	1 medium
• lettuce	5 large leaves	5 large leaves
• tomato	1 medium	1 medium
• green onions	4	4
• whole wheat bun (small)	1	1
• arrowroot biscuits	3	3

Peanut Butter & Banana Sandwich

I never seem to get tired of peanut butter and banana sandwiches.

Peanut butter also goes well with jam or honey. Limit the jam or honey to 1 teaspoon (5 mL), or 2 teaspoons (10 mL) of diet jam. Still have ½ banana or any other fruit choice on the side.

Choose vegetable juice and carrot sticks as shown, or other fresh vegetables.

You may have either ¾ cup (175 mL) of light yogurt or 1 cup (250 mL) of low-fat milk.

My dad's favorite Sunday lunch is a peanut butter and onion sandwich. If you like onions, use as many as you like on your peanut butter sandwich. Then have your fruit on the side.

Yogurt ideas:
- Regular fruit-flavored yogurt may have 3 or more teaspoons (15 mL) of sugar added in ½ cup (125 mL). A yogurt made with a low-calorie sweetener will cut out this extra sugar.
- Mix one container of plain skim milk yogurt with one container of regular fruit yogurt. It will then have 1½ teaspoons (7 mL) of sugar in ½ cup (125 mL).
- Make up your own fruit yogurt simply by adding fruit to a low-fat plain yogurt. Add a low-calorie sweetener if you like.

Food Choices	Large Meal	Small Meal
Carbohydrate	4½	3½
Meat and Alternatives	1	½
Nutritional Info	**Large Meal**	**Small Meal**
Carbohydrate	87 g	69 g
Fiber	7 g	5 g

Your Lunch Menu	Large Meal (520 calories)	Small Meal (400 calories)
Peanut butter & banana sandwich	1½ sandwiches	1 sandwich
• white bread	• 3 slices	• 2 slices
• peanut butter	• 2 tbsp (25 mL)	• 1 tbsp (15 mL)
• small banana	• ½	• ½
Carrot sticks	1 medium carrot	1 medium carrot
Tomato or vegetable juice	½ cup (125 mL)	½ cup (125 mL)
Low-fat yogurt (sweetened with low-calorie sweetener)	¾ cup (175 mL)	¾ cup (175 mL)

SMALL MEAL

Pita Sandwich

Fill your pita with lots of vegetables and a little protein.

Try these vegetables in your pita:
- lettuce and tomatoes
- bean sprouts and alfalfa sprouts
- grated carrots
- chopped green pepper

Try one of these in your pita instead of the cheese and ham
(portions are for the large meal):
- $\frac{1}{2}$ cup (125 mL) water-packed tuna or salmon
- $\frac{1}{2}$ cup (125 mL) 1% cottage cheese
- 3 oz (85 g) firm tofu, chopped
- 2 tbsp (25 mL) peanut butter

Include milk or some other milk food, such as yogurt or a diet ice cream bar.

Food Choices	Large Meal	Small Meal
Carbohydrate	4	3
Meat and Alternatives	2	1$\frac{1}{2}$
Nutritional Info	Large Meal	Small Meal
Carbohydrate	74 g	56 g
Fiber	6 g	4 g

Your Lunch Menu	Large Meal (520 calories)	Small Meal (400 calories)
Pita	1 (6 inches/15 cm)	1 (6 inches/15 cm)
• lettuce	$\frac{1}{4}$ cup (60 mL) chopped	$\frac{1}{4}$ cup (60 mL) chopped
• tomato	$\frac{1}{2}$ medium	$\frac{1}{2}$ medium
• bean sprouts	$\frac{1}{4}$ cup (60 mL)	$\frac{1}{4}$ cup (60 mL)
• carrots	$\frac{1}{2}$ small	$\frac{1}{2}$ small
• green pepper	2 tbsp (25 mL) chopped	2 tbsp (25 mL) chopped
• ham, lean	1 oz (30 g)	1 oz (30 g)
• cheddar cheese, shredded	$\frac{1}{4}$ cup (60 mL)	2 tbsp (25 mL)
Plums	2 medium	1 medium
Skim or 1% milk	$\frac{1}{2}$ cup (125 mL)	$\frac{1}{2}$ cup (125 mL)
Gingersnap cookies	2	–

LUNCH 9

Chef's Salad, Bun & Soup

When you order a salad in a restaurant, ask for low-fat salad dressing on the side. If you don't, your salad will come soaked in fat and will be just as greasy as your neighbor's order of fries.

In restaurants, salads often are served with greasy garlic toast. Ask for a plain bun or dried bread sticks instead.

Whether you're at home or in a restaurant, you may want to have a salad with a bun and soup for your lunch.

A chef's salad recipe follows, and there is a recipe for Citrus Vinaigrette on page 137.

Chef's Salad

Makes 2 servings

2 cups (500 mL) chopped lettuce

2 medium tomatoes, sliced

Other vegetables, such as onions, green peppers, celery, radishes or carrots

1 apple, sliced

2 slices (2 oz/60 g) sliced chicken, meat or cheese, or fish

2 eggs, hard boiled and sliced

2 tbsp (25 mL) low-fat croutons

Per serving	
Calories	243
Carbohydrate	21 g
Fiber	4 g
Protein	13 g
Fat, total	13 g
Fat, saturated	6 g
Cholesterol	208 mg
Sodium	229 mg

1. Toss vegetables and apple. Place the meat or cheese and egg on top. Add croutons.

Food Choices	Large Meal	Small Meal
Carbohydrate	2½	1½
Meat and Alternatives	2	2
Fat	½	½
Nutritional Info	**Large Meal**	**Small Meal**
Carbohydrate	53 g	35 g
Fiber	5 g	4 g

Your Lunch Menu	Large Meal (520 calories)	Small Meal (400 calories)
Cream of mushroom or tomato soup (made with water)	1 cup (250 mL)	reduced-sodium clear broth (optional)
Wheat crackers	2 halves	—
Chef's Salad	1 serving (½ recipe)	1 serving (½ recipe)
Citrus Vinaigrette	2 tbsp (25 mL)	2 tbsp (25 mL)
Bun, white	1 small	1 small
Margarine	½ tsp (2 mL)	½ tsp (2 mL)

SMALL MEAL

French Onion Soup

French onion soup is easy to make at home with this recipe.

Other hearty soups are canned split pea or bean soup, or homemade hamburger soup (see recipe on page 132). Or you could have a bowl of cream soup made with milk and toss in some vegetables.

Another way to make this soup is to use one package of dried onion soup mix (the kind with dried flakes of onion). This package of soup would replace the bouillon and the onions.

There is a lot of salt in soup mix and bouillon. Look for low-salt varieties.

Regular-fat cheese is used in this recipe — as low-fat cheese does not broil as nicely.

French Onion Soup

Makes 4 servings

3 packets (each 4.5 g) reduced-salt beef bouillon mix	
4 cups (1 L) water	
2 medium onions, thinly sliced	
4 slices white bread, toasted	

4 oz (125 g) Swiss or mozzarella cheese (this is equal to 4 slices of cheese, each 4 inches/10 cm square and ⅛ inch/3 mm thick)

Per serving	
Calories	218
Carbohydrate	23 g
Fiber	2 g
Protein	11 g
Fat, total	9 g
Fat, saturated	5 g
Cholesterol	27 mg
Sodium	621 mg

1. Add the bouillon mix, water and sliced onions to a pot. Bring to a boil. Turn down heat and simmer for 15 minutes, until onions are soft.
2. Pour soup into four ovenproof bowls.
3. Cut dry toast into cubes. Put 1 full slice of cubed toast onto each bowl of soup. Place a slice of Swiss cheese on top of the bread.
4. Broil in the oven until the cheese bubbles.

Food Choices	Large Meal	Small Meal
Carbohydrate	3	2
Meat and Alternatives	1	1
Fat	1	–
Nutritional Info	**Large Meal**	**Small Meal**
Carbohydrate	75 g	59 g
Fiber	9 g	7 g

Your Lunch Menu	Large Meal (520 calories)	Small Meal (400 calories)
French Onion Soup	1 serving	1 serving
Tossed salad	Large	Large
Citrus Vinaigrette (page 137)	2 tbsp (25 mL)	2 tbsp (25 mL)
Rye bread	1 slice	–
Margarine	1 tsp (5 mL)	–
Pear	1 medium	1 medium

Quesadilla

A quesadilla (pronounced kay-se-*dee*ya) is a flour tortilla folded in half and lightly fried, with a combination of food in the middle. You can be amazingly creative with every one you make, because the combinations are endless. Include some kind of protein, such as cooked meat, chicken, bacon, canned tuna, canned salmon or beans, along with cheese and salsa, and add either sour cream or light salad dressing.

How big is 1 ounce (30 g) of cheese or meat?

- *cut from a 3½-inch (8.5 cm) block of cheese, it's a ½-inch (1 cm) thick piece*
- *1¼-inch (3 cm) cube of cheese or meat*
- *1 slice from a 4- by 4-inch (10 by 10 cm) package of sliced meat or cheese*
- *⅓ small (5½ oz/ 156 g) can of minced chicken or ham*

Quesadilla

Each quesadilla:

	Per quesadilla
1 8-inch (20 cm) flour tortilla	Calories 300
1 oz (30 g) cooked chicken, ham or beef, sliced or cut into small pieces	Carbohydrate . . . . . 32 g Fiber . . . . 2 g Protein . . . . 16 g
2 tbsp (25 mL) shredded light cheese	Fat, total . . . . 11 g Fat, saturated . . . . . . 4 g
1 tbsp (15 mL) salsa (or several slices of fresh tomato)	Cholesterol . . . . . 40 mg Sodium . . . . 508 mg
½ tsp (2 mL) margarine, olive oil or other vegetable oil	
1 tbsp (15 mL) light sour cream or your favorite light salad dressing	

1. Fold the tortilla in half, then open it up and cover half of the tortilla with the meat, cheese and salsa. Close by folding the top half over.
2. Lightly coat your tortilla with margarine or oil (using a pastry brush, if you have one) and place in a frying pan.
3. Cook over medium heat until lightly browned on both sides.
4. Remove from pan and cut in half or into quarters. Serve with the sour cream or salad dressing on the side.

Food Choices	Large Meal	Small Meal
Carbohydrate	4	3
Meat and Alternatives	2	1½
Nutritional Info	**Large Meal**	**Small Meal**
Carbohydrate	67 g	51 g
Fiber	4 g	3 g

Low-calorie add-ins for your quesadilla:
- a few olives
- sliced onions
- pickled hot peppers or banana peppers
- chopped fresh parsley or cilantro
- honey mustard or regular mustard
- shredded lettuce (add after the quesadilla is cooked)

Your Lunch Menu	Large Meal (520 calories)	Small Meal (400 calories)
Quesadilla Sweet pepper or raw veggies Chocolate pudding, no sugar added	1½ 1 cup (250 mL) 3¾-oz (106 g) container	1 1 cup (250 mL) 3¾-oz (106 g) container

SMALL MEAL

LUNCH 12

Tuna Sandwich

Fish has two great benefits: it is the best source of the most important omega-3 fats, called DHA and EPA, and it is an excellent dietary source of vitamin D. See page 41 for other sources of omega-3 fats.

A tuna sandwich is a smart and easy way to eat one serving of fish. Choose canned fish or leftover mashed fish for your sandwiches. Salmon and sardines are also good choices, and the fish bones give you calcium. Fish and seafood are very nutritious, so try to eat two servings a week. In this book, you'll find six fish or seafood dinners, two lunch meals with fish and several snack ideas to bring fish into your weekly diet.

Alternatives to tuna in your sandwich:
- canned salmon
- canned sardines
- canned or pickled oysters, mussels, kippers or herring

Possible additions to your fish sandwich:
- chopped celery
- chopped or thinly sliced dill pickles
- sliced onion
- alfalfa sprouts
- sliced olives or hot pepper pickles
- green pickle relish
- mustard or horseradish

Serve your sandwich with a glass of skim or 1% milk and a small fruit of your choice.

Flavored tunas

For those of you who are not so fond of fish, you may like the flavored single-serving cans of tuna. One small tin (3 oz/85 g) is equal to half a can of regular tuna. If the tuna is canned in oil, you don't need to add any mayonnaise. Drain off at least half the oil.

Food Choices	Large Meal	Small Meal
Carbohydrate	5	4
Meat and Alternatives	2	1½
Fat	1	½
Nutritional Info	**Large Meal**	**Small Meal**
Carbohydrate	76 g	56 g
Fiber	10 g	7 g

Your Lunch Menu	Large Meal (520 calories)	Small Meal (400 calories)
Tuna sandwich	1½ sandwiches	1 sandwich
• bread	• 3 slices	• 2 slices
• tuna, canned in water, drained	• ⅔ of a 6-oz (170 g) can	• ½ of a 6-oz (170 g) can
• light mayonnaise	• 1 tbsp (15 mL)	• 2 tsp (10 mL)
• chopped celery and alfalfa sprouts	• As desired	• As desired
Skim milk	1 cup (250 mL)	1 cup (250 mL)
Apple	1 small	1 small

SMALL MEAL

Cheese & Crackers

When I'm on my own, I like a quick and easy lunch, so I grab cheese and crackers, an apple and a few pecans or almonds. This is definitely a "no muss, no fuss" lunch.

Although you may be tempted to just eat the crackers, crackers do not supply enough nutrition on their own. When you add cheese to the crackers, you are including both protein and calcium.

Nuts also provide some protein, but more importantly, they have heart-healthy fats and give some interesting variation to your meal. Because of their calories, just a few nuts are included in this lunch.

A fruit or vegetable gives you yet another food group in this simple lunch. If you have a bit more time, you can chop your choice of fruit into bite-size pieces, toss them in a bowl with a teaspoon (5 mL) of grated lemon rind and add a small amount of flavored yogurt. And you can dip your vegetables in a light salad dressing or use one of the vegetable dips shown with Dinner 20.

This lunch is complemented with a cup of hot iced tea (iced tea mix blended with boiling water).

Portions of cheese, crackers and nuts

When choosing your crackers and cheese varieties, keep in mind that manufacturers vary their products and portion sizes, which can change the calories. There are also variations between brand-name and no-name food products. It's a good idea to read the "Nutrition Facts" on the label.

Then select the right portion. For example, for the large meal, 120 calories would be about 12 soda crackers, or 5 Breton-type wheat crackers, or 3 flavored rice cakes, or a combination of these three types.

Food groups

It is recommended that you eat at least three or four food groups at every meal. For information about the food groups, and photographs, see pages 30–41.

Food Choices	Large Meal	Small Meal
Carbohydrate	3½	2½
Meat and Alternatives	1½	1
Fat	1½	1
Nutritional Info	**Large Meal**	**Small Meal**
Carbohydrate	62 g	54 g
Fiber	10 g	9 g

Your Lunch Menu	Large Meal (520 calories)	Small Meal (400 calories)
Cheese	180-calorie portion	120-calorie portion
Crackers	160-calorie portion	110-calorie portion
Fruit	1½ cups (375 mL)	1½ cups (375 mL)
Nuts	75-calorie portion	50-calorie portion
Sugar-free iced tea	1 cup (250 mL)	1 cup (250 mL)

SMALL MEAL

Frozen Entrée or Leftovers

Turn dinner leftovers into an easy lunch
Consider buying reusable microwavable bowls and plates with lids, and use last night's dinner leftovers to make lunch meals that can be frozen and reheated as you need them. These lunch meals will have less salt and additives than store-bought frozen entrées. Store-bought frozen entrées also have extra throwaway packaging. You can help make a difference to the environment by using your own bowls and plates.

Store-bought Frozen Entrées

There are many different kinds of frozen entrées sold in the freezers of your grocery store. They are so convenient, but they may be less nutritious than meals you make yourself. However, they are okay once in a while. To complete your meal and boost your vitamins, be sure to have some raw vegetables on the side and a fruit.

Calorie Guide for Store-Bought Frozen Entrées
For the large meal:
Select a frozen entrée with less than 420 calories
You will be able to choose from a wide variety of the regular meals. Select ones that are lower in fat, sugar and salt. Some of the chicken or beef pot pies are less than 420 calories but have more fat and salt. If you would prefer a light TV dinner under 300 calories, then in addition to your vegetables and fruit, add either a slice of bread or a small bun, a granola bar, pudding or a glass of milk.

For the small meal:
Select a frozen entrée with less than 300 calories
You will need to choose from the light selection of frozen entrées. One pizza pop, pizza pocket or mini pizza will generally be a suitable choice for this calorie range. Remember to include vegetables and a fruit of your choice.

Dinner Leftovers

On pages 106–107 are some dinner meals from this book that can be easily downsized to make a lunch entrée for the next day. Remember, to complete these meals and boost your vitamins, have some raw vegetables and a fruit.

Your Lunch Menu	Large Meal (520 calories)	Small Meal (400 calories)
Frozen entrée or leftovers: • store-bought or • leftovers from dinner Carrots Banana	• up to 420 calories or • portions as shown in chart 10 baby carrots or 1 medium 1 small (or ½ large)	• up to 300 calories or • portions as shown in chart 10 baby carrots or 1 medium 1 small (or ½ large)

SMALL MEAL

Turn Dinner Meals into an Easy Lunch

	Large Lunch Serving of Dinner Leftovers (about 420 calories)	Small Lunch Serving of Dinner Leftovers (about 300 calories)
Dinner 1: Baked chicken Potato Mixed vegetables	3 oz (90 g) 1 medium ½ cup (125 mL)	2 oz (60 g) ½ medium ½ cup (125 mL)
Dinner 2: Cooked spaghetti Spaghetti Meat Sauce	1½ cups (375 mL) ¾ cup (175 mL)	1 cup (250 mL) ½ cup (125 mL)
Dinner 4: Roast beef Horseradish Roasted potatoes Low-Fat Gravy Beets	3 oz (90 g) 2 tsp (10 mL) 1 large 2 tbsp (25 mL) ½ cup (125 mL)	2 oz (60 g) 2 tsp (10 mL) 1 medium 2 tbsp (25 mL) ½ cup (125 mL)
Dinner 6: Hamburger Soup	2¾ cups (675 mL)	2 cups (500 mL)
Dinner 7: Beans & Wieners Tossed salad Citrus Vinaigrette	1 cup (250 mL) Large 1 tbsp (15 mL)	¾ cup (175 mL) Large 1 tbsp (15 mL)
Dinner 10: Baked ham Sweet potato	4 oz (125 g) 1 large	3 oz (90 g) 1 medium
Dinner 11: Beef Stew Boiled potatoes	2 cups (500 mL) ½ medium	1⅓ cups (325 mL) ½ medium
Dinner 13: Sausages Cornbread	4 links 1½ pieces	3 links 1 piece
Dinner 14: Chili Con Carne Rice	1 cup (250 mL) ⅔ cup (150 mL)	¾ cup (175 mL) ⅓ cup (75 mL)
Dinner 15: Perogies Garlic sausage	5 + 1 tsp (5 mL) margarine 1½ oz (45 g)	4 1 oz (30 g)
Dinner 17: Turkey, white Turkey, dark meat Low-Fat Mashed Potatoes Low-Fat Gravy Peas and carrots	2 oz (60 g) 2 oz (60 g) 1 cup (250 mL) ¼ cup (60 mL) ½ cup (125 mL)	3 oz (90 g) – ½ cup (125 mL) ¼ cup (60 mL) ½ cup (125 mL)
Dinner 18: Baked Macaroni & Cheese	1¾ cups (425 mL)	1¼ cups (300 mL)
Dinner 19: Pork chop Applesauce Boiled potatoes with parsley	3 oz (90 g) ¼ cup (60 mL) 6 small	3 oz (90 g) 2 tbsp (25 mL) 3 small

	Large Lunch Serving of Dinner Leftovers (about 420 calories)	Small Lunch Serving of Dinner Leftovers (about 300 calories)
Dinner 20: Bean and Meat Filling Cheese, shredded Brown rice	1 cup (250 mL) 2 tbsp (25 mL) ⅓ cup (75 mL)	¾ cup (175 mL) 2 tbsp (25 mL) ⅓ cup (75 mL)
Dinner 22: Sun Burgers Mixed vegetables	2 burgers 1 cup (250 mL)	1½ burgers ¾ cup (175 mL)
Dinner 24: Hamburger Noodle Dish	1½ cups (375 mL)	1 cup (250 mL)
Dinner 25: Pizza Skim milk	1 large slice 1 cup (250 mL)	1 medium slice 1 cup (250 mL)
Dinner 27: Chinese Stir-Fry Rice	2 cups (500 mL) 1 cup (250 mL)	1½ cups (375 mL) ⅔ cup (150 mL)
Dinner 29: Shish Kebab Rice	1 made with 4 meat cubes ⅔ cup (150 mL)	1 made with 3 meat cubes ⅓ cup (75 mL)
Dinner 30: Curried Chickpeas and Potato Filling	1¼ cups (300 mL)	1 cup less 2 tbsp (225 mL)
Dinner 31: Chicken leg Tandoori Sauce Rice, basmati	2 small ¼ cup (60 mL) ⅓ cup (75 mL)	1 small 2 tbsp (25 mL) ⅓ cup (75 mL)
Dinner 32: Swiss Steak and sauce Potatoes	4 oz (125 g) ½ medium	3 oz (90 g) ½ medium
Dinner 33: Thai Chicken Rice noodles or pasta	1 cup (250 mL) ⅔ cup (150 mL)	¾ cup (175 mL) ⅓ cup (75 mL)
Dinner 36: Beef Parmesan Pasta sauce Cheese, shredded, low-fat Low-Fat Mashed Potatoes	1 patty ¼ cup (60 mL) 2 tbsp (25 mL) ½ cup (125 mL)	1 patty ¼ cup (60 mL) 2 tbsp (25 mL)
Dinner 38: Pork Chop Casserole with sauce Rice	1 chop 1 cup (250 mL)	1 chop ⅔ cup (150 mL)
Dinner 39: Shrimp Linguini Sauce Linguini	1 cup (250 mL) 1 cup (250 mL)	¾ cup (175 mL) ½ cup (125 mL)
Dinner 40: Chicken Cordon Bleu Mashed sweet potato	1 piece ⅓ cup (75 mL)	½ piece ⅔ cup (150 mL)

LUNCH 15

Avocado Salad & Bruschetta

Avocado Salad

Makes 2 servings

2 cups (500 mL) lettuce pieces

1 medium tomato, cut into wedges

1 apple, thinly sliced

1 avocado, sliced

¼ cup (50 mL) shredded light cheese (1 oz/30 g)

Grated lime rind and a drizzle of lime juice

Per ½ recipe	
Calories	268
Carbohydrate	23 g
Fiber	8 g
Protein	7 g
Fat, total	19 g
Fat, saturated	5 g
Cholesterol	10 mg
Sodium	140 mg

1. Toss all ingredients.
2. Top with your favorite low-fat salad dressing.

This is a low-fat version of a traditional Italian bruschetta.

Bruschetta

For each slice:

½-inch (1 cm) slice of French baguette (or ½ slice of regular bread)

1 tsp (5 mL) salsa or low-fat pasta sauce

1 to 2 tsp (5 to 10 mL) of toppings such as:
• sliced olives or capers
• pickled or fresh garlic cloves, chopped or whole
• chopped fresh or dried herbs, such as cilantro, basil or chives

2 tsp (10 mL) thinly sliced, crumbled or shredded light cheese

Per slice	
Calories	40
Carbohydrate	5 g
Fiber	0 g
Protein	2 g
Fat, total	2 g
Fat, saturated	1 g
Cholesterol	2 mg
Sodium	123 mg

1. Place bread pieces on a cookie sheet. Under the grill, toast the top side of the bread slices.
2. Remove cookie sheet from the oven. To each slice of bread add the salsa, toppings and cheese. Put the bread slices back in the oven to grill the cheese.

Food Choices	Large Meal	Small Meal
Carbohydrate	2	1½
Meat and Alternatives	½	½
Fat	4	3½
Nutritional Info	**Large Meal**	**Small Meal**
Carbohydrate	52 g	40 g
Fiber	10 g	9 g

Your Lunch Menu	Large Meal (520 calories)	Small Meal (400 calories)
Avocado Salad Light salad dressing Bruschetta	1 serving 2 tbsp (25 mL) 5 baguette slices	1 serving 1 tbsp (15 mL) 3 baguette slices

SMALL MEAL

Dinner Meals

- **each large dinner has 730 calories**
- **each small dinner has 550 calories**

DINNER 1

Baked Chicken & Potato

The following recipe for **Chicken Spice Mix** *makes enough for many meals. Put 2 teaspoons (10 mL) oregano and 1 teaspoon (5 mL) each thyme, paprika, pepper and chili powder in a jar with a tight lid. Mix well. Sprinkle the mixture on the skinless chicken.*

It is important to remove the fatty chicken skin. Sprinkle on this salt-free and sugar-free Chicken Spice Mix — see sidebar. Or roll the chicken in a store-bought shake-and-bake coating, or baste lightly with your favorite barbecue sauce.

Bake the chicken pieces on a rack so the extra fat drip offs. Bake in a 350°F (180°C) oven for about an hour. Or grill on the barbecue. Or cook in a nonstick pan with a small amount of water and barbecue sauce. Chicken is cooked when the meat moves easily when pierced with a fork, and the juices have no trace of pink. Or cook to 170°F (75°C) measured with an instant-read thermometer.

Compare the fat and sugar content of fast-food chicken with this home-baked chicken, which has the skin and fat removed.

The breast of baked chicken shown in the **small** meal photograph has:
- 1 teaspoon (5 mL) of fat
- no sugar

The same piece of chicken, if battered and deep-fried at a fast-food restaurant, would have:
- 4 teaspoons (20 mL) of fat
- 3 teaspoons (15 mL) of sugar or starch

Have your potato plain, with 1 teaspoon (5 mL) of butter or margarine, or with 1 tablespoon (15 mL) of light or fat-free sour cream.

The vegetables that go with this meal are celery, radishes and frozen mixed vegetables.

Easy-to-make pudding from a box:
Light puddings sweetened with a low-calorie sweetener are often marked as "fat-free." You can tell they are diet mixes because they are a lot lighter in weight than the regular. The same is true for diet gelatin. They are a good source of calcium and have fewer calories than regular puddings. Make your puddings with skim milk. Butterscotch pudding has been chosen for this meal, but you can choose your own favorite flavor.

Instead of frozen mixed vegetables, you could choose one of these sweet vegetables:
- *peas*
- *carrots*
- *parsnips*
- *beets*
- *turnips*
- *squash (orange)*

Store-bought light puddings or light mousses should have fewer than 75 calories in a 1/2-cup (125 mL) serving.

Instead of pudding, you could choose 1 cup (250 mL) low-fat milk.

Food Choices	Large Meal	Small Meal
Carbohydrate	4	3
Meat and Alternatives	5	3½
Nutritional Info	**Large Meal**	**Small Meal**
Carbohydrate	89 g	72 g
Fiber	10 g	9 g

Your Dinner Menu	Large Meal (730 calories)	Small Meal (550 calories)
Baked chicken	1½ breasts (5 oz/150 g, cooked)	1 breast (3½ oz/100 g, cooked)
Baked potato, with skin	1 large or 1½ medium	1 medium
Light sour cream	1½ tbsp (22 mL)	1 tbsp (15 mL)
Mixed vegetables	¾ cup (175 mL)	¾ cup (175 mL)
Radishes	4	4
Celery	1 stalk	1 stalk
Light butterscotch pudding	½ cup (125 mL)	½ cup (125 mL)

SMALL MEAL

DINNER 2

Spaghetti & Meat Sauce

Spaghetti and meat sauce is an easy-to-make favorite. I often double this recipe and freeze the extra. When you have no dinner planned, it's great to have a container of spaghetti sauce in the freezer.

Spaghetti Meat Sauce

Makes 6 cups (1.5 L) of sauce

1 lb (500 g) lean ground beef

1 medium onion, chopped

28 oz (796 mL) can tomatoes

1 cup (250 mL) water

1 small tin (5½ oz/156 mL) tomato paste

½ tsp (2 mL) garlic powder or 2 cloves garlic, chopped

2 bay leaves (remove before serving)

½ tsp (2 mL) chili powder

1 tsp (5 mL) dried oregano

1 tsp (5 mL) dried basil

¼ tsp (1 mL) paprika

⅛ tsp (0.5 mL) ground cinnamon

⅛ tsp (0.5 mL) ground cloves

1 cup (250 mL) chopped vegetables, such as green pepper, celery or mushrooms

Per 1 cup (250 mL)	
Calories	200
Carbohydrate	17 g
Fiber	4 g
Protein	17 g
Fat, total	8 g
Fat, saturated	3 g
Cholesterol	40 mg
Sodium	296 mg

1. Brown the ground beef. Drain off as much fat as you can.
2. Add the rest of the ingredients.
3. Bring to a boil, then turn down heat. Cover and simmer for about 1 hour. Stir every now and then so the sauce doesn't stick. Add extra water if it gets too thick.
4. Serve over hot spaghetti, with parmesan cheese if you like.

Use regular or whole wheat spaghetti. Add dry spaghetti to a pot of boiling water, stir and cook for about 10 minutes. Drain off water.

Whether you use regular or lean ground beef, it is important to brown it first and drain off as much fat as you can.

You can remove extra fat by adding hot water to the browned meat, then draining it off.

For a meatless spaghetti sauce, make this recipe according to the directions but do not add the ground beef (omit step 1). For protein for the large meal, sprinkle 5 tablespoons (75 mL) of shredded cheese or 3 tablespoons (45 mL) of sunflower seeds or chopped nuts on top of your cooked spaghetti and sauce. Use a little less for the small meal.

Store-bought spaghetti sauces (in jars or cans) can have a lot of added fat, sugar, salt or starch. For example, 1 cup (250 mL) of some meatless spaghetti sauces have 2 teaspoons (10 mL) of added fat and 4 teaspoons (20 mL) of added sugar or starch. If you do buy spaghetti sauce, look for one labeled as "light."

Carrots are served with this meal.

Use an oil-free salad dressing. See Dinner 7, page 136, for more about low-fat salad dressings.

Light gelatin has few calories and is a good dessert choice after a big meal. It takes only a few minutes to make, but must be left in the fridge for about 2 hours to set. If you find the boxed diet gelatins are costly, try this easy-to-make recipe.

Light Gelatin

Makes 2 cups (500 mL)

1 envelope ($\frac{1}{4}$ oz/7 g) unflavored gelatin

$\frac{1}{2}$ package regular drink mix
(such as Kool-Aid)

1 cup (250 mL) cold water

1 cup (250 mL) boiling water

Low-calorie sweetener equal to $\frac{1}{4}$ cup (50 mL) sugar
(use a bit less or more, to suit your taste)

Per $\frac{1}{2}$ cup (125 mL)	
Calories	13
Carbohydrate	2 g
Fiber	0 g
Protein	2 g
Fat, total	0 g
Fat, saturated	0 g
Cholesterol	0 mg
Sodium	19 mg

1. Soften the unflavored gelatin in $\frac{1}{2}$ cup (125 mL) cold water.
2. Add the drink mix and 1 cup (250 mL) boiling water. Stir until gelatin is all mixed in.
3. Add $\frac{1}{2}$ cup (125 mL) cold water and low-calorie sweetener.
4. Chill until firm (about 2 hours).

*W*hipped Gelatin is a variation you may want to try (see Dinner 10, page 149). When you whip the gelatin, you will get 4 cups (1 L) instead of 2 cups (500 mL).

*A*nother low-calorie dessert is store-bought "no sugar added" popsicles.

Food Choices	Large Meal	Small Meal
Carbohydrate	5	4
Meat and Alternatives	$2\frac{1}{2}$	$1\frac{1}{2}$

Nutritional Info	Large Meal	Small Meal
Carbohydrate	113 g	96 g
Fiber	10	8 g

Your Dinner Menu	Large Meal (730 calories)	Small Meal (550 calories)
Spaghetti, cooked	$1\frac{1}{2}$ cups (375 mL)	$1\frac{1}{2}$ cups (375 mL)
Meat sauce	$1\frac{1}{4}$ cups (300 mL)	$\frac{3}{4}$ cup (175 mL)
Cooked carrots	$\frac{1}{2}$ cup (125 mL)	$\frac{1}{2}$ cup (125 mL)
Salad	Medium	Medium
Oil-free salad dressing	1 tbsp (15 mL)	1 tbsp (15 mL)
Skim or 1% milk	1 cup (250 mL)	$\frac{1}{2}$ cup (125 mL)
Light gelatin	$\frac{1}{2}$ cup (125 mL)	$\frac{1}{2}$ cup (125 mL)

SMALL MEAL

DINNER *3*

Low-fat fish:
- *bluefish*
- *catfish*
- *cod*
- *haddock*
- *perch*
- *pickerel*
- *red snapper*
- *sole*
- *tilapia*

High-fat fish (good sources of healthy omega-3 fats):
- *mackerel*
- *salmon*
- *sardines*
- *trout*
- *tuna*
Eat a bit less of the high-fat fish.

These spices go well with fish:
- *allspice*
- *basil*
- *Cajun spice*
- *curry*
- *dill*
- *mustard*
- *oregano*
- *parsley*
- *thyme*

Fish with Rice

The fish may be broiled or baked in an oven at 350°F to 400°F (180°C to 200°C). The fish shown in the photograph is red snapper, and it was baked and lightly brushed with margarine. Fish can also be microwaved, steamed, grilled on the barbecue, or fried in a nonstick pan (with just a little fat). If you are cooking fish in your oven or on your barbecue, you can wrap it in foil. Fish is good with spices, onions and vegetables wrapped up in the foil too.

Before cooking fish:
Poke it with a fork and pour 2 tablespoons (25 mL) of lemon juice or ¼ cup (50 mL) of dry wine over it. Sprinkle it with your favorite spices. You may also want to roll the fish in bread crumbs or flour.

The secret to great-tasting fish is to not overcook it. Fish is cooked when it flakes easily.

Rice:
Cook rice according to directions on the package, omitting any salt.

If you're pressed for time, you can substitute 3 slices of whole-grain bread for 1 cup (250 mL) of rice.

Cooked white and brown rice both have about 210 calories per cup (250 mL). Brown rice, however, is a better choice as it has almost 3 grams of fiber per cup, while white rice has just over half a gram.

Vegetables:
This meal is served with peas, a sweet vegetable, and with yellow or green beans, which are less sweet. See page 149 for a list of low-calorie vegetables.

Fruit Milkshake

Makes 2 cups (500 mL)

1 cup (250 mL) skim milk

½ cup (125 mL) frozen or fresh fruit
of your choice

1 tbsp (15 mL) sugar or equal amount
of low-calorie sweetener

Per 1 cup (250 mL)	
Calories	79
Carbohydrate	16 g
Fiber	1 g
Protein	4 g
Fat, total	0 g
Fat, saturated	0 g
Cholesterol	2 mg
Sodium	52 mg

1. Pour the milk in a mixing bowl or a blender. Place your mixing bowl or blender in your freezer for 30 minutes.
2. Take your bowl or blender out of the freezer. Add the fruit and sugar (or low-calorie sweetener) to the milk. Mix in the blender for about 30 seconds. If you don't have a blender, mix in your bowl with beaters until thick and frothy. Serve right away.

This milkshake is easy to make. It is so thick and good, you won't believe it's made with skim milk and not with ice cream.

If you increase the size of the recipe, you will need to freeze it for longer.

Food Choices	Large Meal	Small Meal
Carbohydrate	4½	3½
Meat and Alternatives	6	4
Fat	1	1
Nutritional Info	**Large Meal**	**Small Meal**
Carbohydrate	94 g	79 g
Fiber	13 g	12 g

Your Dinner Menu	Large Meal (730 calories)	Small Meal (550 calories)
Fish with lemon slice	6 oz (175 g), cooked	4 oz (125 g), cooked
Margarine (to cook fish)	1 tsp (5 mL)	1 tsp (5 mL)
Brown rice, cooked	1 cup (250 mL)	⅔ cup (150 mL)
Green peas	½ cup (2 mL)	½ cup (2 mL)
Yellow beans	1 cup (250 mL)	1 cup (250 mL)
Fruit Milkshake	1 cup (250 mL)	1 cup (250 mL)
Kiwi	1 medium	1 medium

SMALL MEAL

Roast Beef

Here's a great way to cook your roast:

- Place your roast on a rack in a roasting pan, with no lid. Add 1 cup (250 mL) of water to the pan. Sprinkle with pepper but not salt (salt tends to dry out the roast). Bake in a hot 500°F (260°C) oven for 30 minutes.
- Reduce the oven heat to 275°F (140°C). Leave roast uncovered and cook for another $1\frac{1}{2}$ hours for a 5-pound (2.4 kg) roast.

Once the roast beef has been removed from the pan, skim the fat from the meat juice with a spoon. Or put some ice cubes into the meat juice, and the fat will stick to the ice cubes. With a spoon, take out the ice cubes. If you have time, you can let the juice cool and the fat in the juice will harden and can then easily be removed. You can serve the meat juice as it is, or thicken it into a gravy as below.

The lower-cost, medium-tender, low-fat cuts of roast beef are:
- *"round" cuts, such as inside round and outside round*
- *"loin" cuts, such as sirloin or sirloin tip*

Roast beef can also be cooked in a table-top "slow cooker" pot.

You can also buy low-fat gravy mix packages, to which you add only water. These should have fewer than 10 calories in a serving. Look for one that says it is low in calories; it may be called "au jus" (with juice).

Use homemade broth for gravy to reduce salt.

Gravy flavorings:
- *mushrooms*
- *hot sauce*
- *pepper*
- *Worcestershire sauce*
- *garlic*
- *reduced-salt soy sauce*

Low-Fat Gravy

Makes $2\frac{1}{3}$ cups (575 mL)

	Per $\frac{1}{4}$ cup (60 mL)	
1 to 2 packets (4.5 g each) reduced-salt beef bouillon mix (use chicken bouillon if making gravy for poultry) or 1 tsp (5 mL) onion soup mix	Calories . . . . 22 Carbohydrate . . . . . . 4 g Fiber. . . . . 0 g Protein . . . . 1 g Fat, total . . . . 0 g Fat, saturated . . . . . . 0 g Cholesterol . . . . . . 0 mg Sodium. . . . . 83 mg	
1 tbsp (15 mL) finely chopped onion		

2 cups (500 mL) liquid made from either fat-free meat juice, potato water or other vegetable water

$\frac{1}{4}$ cup (50 mL) flour, cornstarch or instant blending flour

$\frac{1}{2}$ cup (125 mL) cold water

1. Add the beef bouillon and onion to your 2 cups (500 mL) of hot liquid.
2. In a jar, mix the flour or cornstarch with the cold water. Tighten the lid and shake well. Add this mixture slowly to the hot juice and cook at medium heat. Stir it often with a whisk until thick and smooth, about 5 minutes.

The oven-roasted potatoes are peeled and cooked for an hour on a nonstick or greased rack or pan. Coat your potatoes with an oil-free Italian dressing or sprinkle with spices.

Have beets as shown, or carrots, turnips, corn, peas, or any other vegetable.

For dessert have the rhubarb with either a lower-fat ice cream (made with 10% B.F., or butter fat), sherbet, frozen yogurt or ice milk. If you don't want dessert, drink 1 cup (250 mL) of milk with your meal.

*E*njoy horseradish with your roast beef; it is a low-fat relish.

*V*egetables such as carrots are also good baked on a rack in the oven.

*T*his rhubarb is nice as a dessert or as a snack served warm on a piece of toast.

Stewed Rhubarb

Makes 1³⁄₄ cups (425 mL)

4 cups (1 L) rhubarb (fresh or frozen), cut into 1-inch (2.5 cm) pieces

2 tbsp (25 mL) water

½ tsp (2 mL) sugar-free drink mix (either strawberry or raspberry)

Dash of cinnamon

Per 1 cup (250 mL)	
Calories	64
Carbohydrate	15 g
Fiber	5 g
Protein	3 g
Fat, total	1 g
Fat, saturated	0 g
Cholesterol	0 mg
Sodium	21 mg

1. Put the rhubarb and water in a heavy pot and cook at low temperature on the stove. Add water as needed. Cook for about 15 minutes, or until soft.
2. Take off the stove and, while still warm, add sugar-free drink mix and cinnamon.
3. Have it warm or cool. Keep in the fridge.

Food Choices	Large Meal	Small Meal
Carbohydrate	4	3
Meat and Alternatives	5	3
Nutritional Info	**Large Meal**	**Small Meal**
Carbohydrate	92 g	76 g
Fiber	13 g	11 g

Your Dinner Menu	Large Meal (730 calories)	Small Meal (550 calories)
Roast beef	5 oz (150 g), cooked	3 oz (90 g), cooked
Horseradish	1 tbsp (15 mL)	1 tbsp (15 mL)
Baked onions	3 small or 1 medium	3 small or 1 medium
Roasted potatoes	1 large	1 medium
Low-Fat Gravy	¼ cup (60 mL)	2 tbsp (25 mL)
Beets	½ cup (125 mL)	½ cup (125 mL)
Salad	Small	Small
Oil-free Italian salad dressing	1 tbsp (15 mL)	1 tbsp (15 mL)
Stewed Rhubarb	1 cup (250 mL)	1 cup (250 mL)
Ice Cream	¼ cup (60 mL)	¼ cup (60 mL)

SMALL MEAL

DINNER *5*

Dinner Cold Plate

This is one of my mom's favorite light and easy meals.

You may wish to replace the cheese shown in the photograph with low-fat cheese (see side bar).

Fish choices include canned (or leftover cooked and chilled) salmon, tuna, sardines, shrimp, crab or lobster. Red (sockeye) salmon is included with this meal. You may want to choose pink salmon, which is a bit lower in fat than red. You may have 1 slice of cold meat instead of fish.

Your starch may be a whole wheat bun, 2 slices of whole-grain bread, or 8 melba toasts. Add any number and variety of fresh vegetables.

You can replace 2 ounces (60 g) of regular-fat cheese (32% fat) with:
- *the same amount of low-fat (17% fat) cheese*
- *¹/₂ cup (125 mL) of 1% cottage cheese*

For dessert have this rice pudding. The pudding is not too creamy but has a nice cinnamon flavor and is the right sweetness. It is good warm or cold.

Rice Pudding

Makes four 1-cup (250 mL) servings

Ingredients	Per 1 cup (250 mL)
1 egg	Calories 216
1½ cups (375 mL) skim milk	Carbohydrate . . . . . 42 g
2 tbsp (25 mL) sugar (or low-calorie sweetener, if desired)	Fiber . . . . 2 g Protein . . . . 8 g
½ tsp (2 mL) ground cinnamon	Fat, total . . . . 2 g Fat, saturated . . . . . . 1 g
½ tsp (2 mL) vanilla	Cholesterol . . . . . 48 mg
2 cups (500 mL) cooked rice (brown or white)	Sodium . . . . 69 mg
¼ cup (50 mL) raisins	

1. In a large bowl, beat the egg, milk, sugar or sweetener, cinnamon and vanilla. Use a spoon or whisk.
2. Stir in rice and raisins.
3. Pour into lightly greased baking dish.
4. Bake at 350°F (180°C) for 45 minutes, or until the center is set.

Instead of the rice pudding you could have a slice of banana bread, light pudding, a small dish of sherbet or frozen yogurt, or a serving of fresh fruit.

Food Choices	Large Meal	Small Meal
Carbohydrate	4	3½
Meat and Alternatives	4	3
Fat	½	–
Nutritional Info	Large Meal	Small Meal
Carbohydrate	73 g	63 g
Fiber	8 g	7 g

Your Dinner Menu	Large Meal (730 calories)	Small Meal (550 calories)
Dinner Cold Plate		
• lettuce or spinach	A plateful	A plateful
• tomato	½ medium	½ medium
• green & red pepper	5 rings	5 rings
• cucumber	4 thick slices	4 thick slices
• radishes	2 large	2 large
• salmon	½ cup (125 mL)	½ cup (125 mL)
• cheddar cheese	2 oz (60 g)	1 oz (30 g)
• bun, whole wheat	1	1
• margarine	½ tsp (2 mL)	–
Rice Pudding	1 cup (250 mL)	¾ cup (175 mL)

SMALL MEAL

Hamburger Soup & Bannock

This delicious meal is a favorite among Canadian Aboriginal people. The great thing about this soup is that it is a meal all in one. Freeze any leftovers.

Canned vegetables and soup contain a lot of sodium, so you do not need to add salt to recipes that use them. If you are able to buy reduced-salt or low-sodium versions, such as tomato soup with 25% less salt or low-sodium canned tomatoes, they are good choices. In addition, plain frozen vegetables, such as frozen corn, have much less sodium than canned.

Hamburger Soup

Makes 10 cups (2.5 L)

Per 1½ cups (375 mL)	
Calories	229
Carbohydrate	27 g
Fiber	3 g
Protein	16 g
Fat, total	7 g
Fat, saturated	3 g
Cholesterol	36 mg
Sodium	456 mg

1 lb (500 g) lean ground beef (or chopped or ground wild meat)
1 medium onion, chopped
4 cloves garlic or 1 tsp (5 mL) garlic powder
19 oz (540 mL) can tomatoes
10 oz (284 mL) can tomato soup
1 tsp (5 mL) Worcestershire sauce
¼ tsp (1 mL) pepper
4 cups (1 L) water
½-1 packet (2.25 to 4.5 g) reduced-salt beef bouillon mix
3 medium carrots, peeled and sliced
1 cup (250 mL) chopped cabbage
1½ cups (375 mL) frozen corn or 12 oz (341 mL) can corn kernels
¼ cup (50 mL) dry macaroni

1. Brown the hamburger meat. Drain off as much fat as you can.
2. Add the onions and garlic, and cook at low heat until onions are soft.
3. Add the tomatoes, tomato soup, Worcestershire sauce, pepper, water and bouillon mix.
4. Bring to a boil, cover and simmer for 30 minutes.
5. Add the vegetables and macaroni. Cover and simmer for another 30 minutes.

If you've never had bannock — try it. This bread is made without yeast and is easy to make. It is cooked in the oven or in a cast-iron frying pan. Instead of the piece of bannock shown here, you may choose 2 slices of bread or 1 bun.

Bannock

Makes one 9-inch (23 cm) bannock (or 10 pieces)

3 cups (750 mL) flour

1½ tsp (7 mL) baking powder

½ tsp (2 mL) salt

1 tbsp (15 mL) sugar

¼ cup (50 mL) vegetable oil, or margarine or other fat, melted

1¼ cups (300 mL) skim milk

Per 1 piece	
Calories	201
Carbohydrate	31 g
Fiber	1 g
Protein	5 g
Fat, total	6 g
Fat, saturated	0 g
Cholesterol	0 mg
Sodium	172 mg

1. In a large bowl, mix together the flour, baking powder, salt and sugar.
2. Mix the vegetable oil with the milk. Add this mixture to the flour. Mix with a spoon to make a soft dough.
3. Put this on a floured board or table. With your hands, flatten and shape it until it is one 9-inch (23 cm) piece.
4. Put on a nonstick or lightly greased cookie sheet. Bake in the oven at 375°F (190°C) for 20 minutes, or until lightly browned.
5. Cut into 10 pieces.

Here's how you can cook bannock on your stove or campfire. Make the bannock batter with only 2 tablespoons (25 mL) of margarine or other fat. Add an extra tablespoon (15 mL) of milk to keep the batter soft. Into the cast-iron pan, add 2 tablespoons (25 mL) fat and fry the bannock for 10 minutes on each side at low heat. This fried bannock has the same amount of fat as it does when baked.

You can use any type of fat when you make bannock. I prefer to use margarine because it gives the bannock a nice golden color.

I use milk instead of water in the bannock because the milk helps in the rising, adding flavor and good nutrition too.

Bannock is nice when ¼ cup (50 mL) of raisins or blueberries are added to the batter.

Food Choices	Large Meal	Small Meal
Carbohydrate	6	4½
Meat and Alternatives	1½	1½
Fat	3	2
Nutritional Info	**Large Meal**	**Small Meal**
Carbohydrate	106 g	74 g
Fiber	8 g	7 g

Your Dinner Menu	Large Meal (730 calories)	Small Meal (550 calories)
Hamburger Soup	1½ cups (375 mL)	1½ cups (375 mL)
Bannock	2 pieces	1 piece
Margarine	1 tsp (5 mL)	1 tsp (5 mL)
Orange	1 medium	1 medium

SMALL MEAL

Beans & Wieners

Beef or pork wieners are high in fat and salt. This meal makes a few wieners go a long way. The beans are low-fat and give you protein and fiber.

Try a lower-fat wiener such as a turkey wiener. A tofu wiener is a vegetarian choice and is even lower in fat. Tofu is made from soy beans, which are low in fat and high in protein. You will usually find tofu and tofu wieners in the vegetable section of your grocery store.

You can also make Beans & Wieners by combining a 14-oz (398 mL) can of brown beans in tomato sauce with 2 chopped wieners. This will make enough for 1 large serving and 1 small serving. Don't forget that canned beans contain a lot of sodium — about 850 mg per cup (250 mL). Home-Baked Beans are a healthier choice, at just 157 mg per cup.

Home-Baked Beans

Makes 4½ cups (1.125 L)

	Per 1 cup (250 mL)	
2 cups (500 mL) dry white beans (navy, small white or Great Northern)	Calories 364	
	Carbohydrate ..... 69 g	
1 medium onion, chopped	Fiber .... 15 g	
	Protein .... 20 g	
2 cloves garlic, finely chopped	Fat, total .... 2 g	
	Fat, saturated ..... 0 g	
1 tbsp (15 mL) dry mustard	Cholesterol ...... 0 mg	
¼ tsp (1 mL) black pepper	Sodium .... 157 mg	
2 cups (500 mL) water		
3 tbsp (45 mL) ketchup		
2 tbsp (25 mL) molasses		
Dash of hot pepper sauce (optional)		

1. Rinse the beans in cold water, removing any shriveled or discolored beans. Place in a pot with enough cold water to cover the beans. Cover and bring to a boil over high heat; boil for 5 minutes. Remove from heat and let stand, covered, for 1 hour.
2. Drain the water from the beans and transfer beans to a casserole dish or bean pot. Mix in the remaining ingredients. Cover and bake at 275°F (140°C) for 6 to 8 hours, or until beans are tender. Stir periodically and add extra water if the beans are drying out.

Beans & Wieners

Makes 3½ cups (875 mL)

	Per 1½ cups (375 mL)
3 cups (750 mL) Home-Baked Beans	Calories 372
	Carbohydrate ..... 61 g
2 regular wieners (each wiener weighs 1½ oz/45 g or less)	Fiber .... 13 g
	Protein .... 20 g
	Fat, total .... 7 g
	Fat, saturated ...... 2 g
	Cholesterol ..... 13 mg
	Sodium .... 333 mg

1. Place the beans in a pot or cooking dish.
2. Cut the wieners in slices and add to the beans.
3. Heat on the stove or in a microwave oven.

Serve Beans & Wieners with toast and a tossed salad, with a low-fat or fat-free salad dressing (look for the words "fat-free," "oil-free" or "calorie-reduced" on the label). Look for salad dressings that have fewer than 25 calories per tablespoon (15 mL). Some regular salad dressings have more than 100 calories per tablespoon.

When choosing salad dressings, remember that they are often very high in sodium. Citrus Vinaigrette is an easy low-fat alternative to store-bought, and contains only 25 mg of sodium per tablespoon (15 mL), compared with over 200 mg in a typical fat-free dressing.

If you want to lower the carbohydrate in this meal, omit one or both slices of toast.

You may want to make the chocolate mousse with regular pudding instead of light. By doing so, you will add an extra 2½ teaspoons (12 mL) of sugar to each serving.

Citrus Vinaigrette

In a large jar (at least 16 oz/500 mL), combine ½ cup (125 mL) orange juice, ¼ cup (50 mL) water, ¼ cup (50 mL) vinegar, 2 tbsp (25 mL) honey, 2 tbsp (25 mL) lemon juice, ¼ tsp (1 mL) garlic powder, ¼ tsp (1 mL) salt and a dash of hot pepper sauce (optional). Shake well and store in the refrigerator for up to 7 days. Makes 1½ cups (375 mL).

This dessert recipe is easy, thick and delicious.

Chocolate Mousse

Makes six ½-cup (125 mL) servings.

1½ cups (375 mL) skim milk

1 package (4-serving size) of light chocolate instant pudding mix

1 cup (250 mL) frozen light whipped topping, thawed until soft

Per ½ cup (125 mL)
Calories 79
Carbohydrate ..... 11 g
Fiber .... 1 g
Protein .... 3 g
Fat, total .... 2 g
Fat, saturated ...... 2 g
Cholesterol ...... 1 mg
Sodium .... 253 mg

1. Pour the skim milk into a medium bowl and add the pudding mix. Beat with a whisk or an electric mixer until thickened (about 2 minutes).
2. Fold in the thawed whipped topping until well blended (or if you want a marbled look, fold in the topping gently and don't fully mix). Pour into six dessert dishes, and serve.

Food Choices	Large Meal	Small Meal
Carbohydrate	5	4
Meat and Alternatives	3	2
Fat	½	–
Nutritional Info	Large Meal	Small Meal
Carbohydrate	123 g	95 g
Fiber	21 g	14 g

Your Dinner Menu	Large Meal (730 calories)	Small Meal (550 calories)
Beans & Wieners	1½ cups (375 mL)	1 cup (250 mL)
Toast	2 small or 1 regular slice	2 small or 1 regular slice
Margarine	½ tsp (2 mL)	–
Tossed salad	Large	Large
Citrus Vinaigrette	2 tbsp (25 mL)	2 tbsp (25 mL)
Chocolate Mousse	½ cup (125 mL)	½ cup (125 mL)

SMALL MEAL

Steak & Potato

The simplest way to cook a steak is to barbecue or broil it, or fry it in a very hot, heavy frying pan with a bit of water. If frying in a pan, cover with a lid to reduce fat spraying out. Cook for only about 4 minutes on each side.

Tips to make your steak more tasty and tender:
- Marinate your meat for a few hours in Shish Kebab Marinade (see page 224) — then barbecue or broil it.
- Soak it for a few hours in canned tomatoes, wine, wine vinegar, beer or plain yogurt. Then fry the steak in a bit of broth or water, or barbecue or broil it.
- Brown the steak on the stove in a bit of beef broth or water. Add canned tomatoes or salsa. Cover the pan and simmer for 1 hour.

Fresh mushrooms can be barbecued or broiled. Canned or fresh mushrooms can be cooked in a separate pan or added to the pan with the steak.

Serve the steak with Low-Fat Mashed Potatoes or with a boiled or baked potato.

Look for "round" or "loin" cuts of beef. These are lowest in fat and are less costly.

Trim off all the fat.

On the barbecue, try not to let your meat burn. You can stop this by lightly spraying the coals with water to keep the flames down.

Make low-fat mashed potatoes by mashing the potatoes and adding only milk, no butter or margarine. Add enough milk to make the potatoes creamy and smooth.

Low-Fat Mashed Potatoes

Makes 2 cups (500 mL)

3 medium potatoes (about 1 lb/500 g)
1/3 cup (75 mL) skim or 1% milk

1. Wash and peel potatoes and cut into quarters.
2. Place potatoes in a large pot with enough water to cover. Bring to a boil, then reduce heat, cover and boil gently for about 20 minutes or until fork-tender.
3. Remove from heat, add milk and mash.

Per 1/2 cup (125 mL)	
Calories	86
Carbohydrate	19 g
Fiber	1 g
Protein	2 g
Fat, total	0 g
Fat, saturated	0 g
Cholesterol	0 mg
Sodium	13 mg

Spice Mix

Here is a spice mix you can make.
Shake some on your meat, your potato
or rice, and your vegetable.

Per ¼ tsp (1 mL)	
Calories	2
Carbohydrate	0 g
Fiber	0 g
Protein	0 g
Fat, total	0 g
Fat, saturated	0 g
Cholesterol	0 mg
Sodium	1 mg

2 tsp (10 mL) garlic powder
1 tsp (5 mL) dried basil
1 tsp (5 mL) dried oregano
1 tsp (5 mL) ground pepper
1 tsp (5 mL) chili powder

*Does your food taste
bland without the
extra shake of salt?
If so, try some of these
on your meat, potato
or vegetables:*
- *pepper*
- *parsley (fresh or
  dried)*
- *lemon or lime juice*
- *onion powder*
- *garlic powder*
- *spices or herbs*
- *store-bought spice
  mixes*

Choose an oil-free or fat-free salad dressing for your salad.

Brussels sprouts are healthy mini cabbages. If you don't have
any, choose one of your own favorite vegetables.

Sherbet, frozen yogurt, ice milk and 10% B.F. ice cream
have less fat than regular ice cream. Here's a little trick to help
your smaller dessert portion seem like more: portion out your
sherbet with a melon baller.

Food Choices	Large Meal	Small Meal
Carbohydrate	3½	2
Meat and Alternatives	5	3

Nutritional Info	Large Meal	Small Meal
Carbohydrate	86 g	67 g
Fiber	11 g	10 g

Your Dinner Menu	Large Meal (730 calories)	Small Meal (550 calories)
Steak	5 oz (150 g), cooked	3 oz (90 g), cooked
Low-Fat Mashed Potatoes	1 cup (250 mL)	½ cup (125 mL)
Mushrooms	½ cup (125 mL)	½ cup (125 mL)
Brussels sprouts	¾ cup (175 mL)	¾ cup (175 mL)
Salad	Large	Large
Oil-free salad dressing	1 tbsp (15 mL)	1 tbsp (15 mL)
Sherbet	½ cup (125 mL)	½ cup (125 mL)

SMALL MEAL

DINNER 9

Cheese Omelet

An omelet makes a great dinner. I cook a cheese omelet about once a week because it is easy and fast. It is okay to have eggs for a main meal once a week, as long as the eggs are eaten in place of meat.

Cheese Omelet

This is the recipe for the small meal. The large meal serving is the same, but it is made with 2 eggs.

1 egg

1 oz (30 g) (or 1 slice) cheese, cut into pieces

Per small omelet	
Calories	187
Carbohydrate	1 g
Fiber	0 g
Protein	13 g
Fat, total	14 g
Fat, saturated	8 g
Cholesterol	216 mg
Sodium	237 mg

1. In a small bowl, beat the eggs. Pour into a nonstick pan.
2. Place the cheese on top.
3. Put a lid on and cook at low heat, for about 5 minutes.

To your broccoli, you may add 1 tablespoon (15 mL) of light cheese spread. This has the same calories as 1 teaspoon (5 mL) of butter or margarine.

For dessert, enjoy 1 or 2 oatmeal cookies. Or in place of an oatmeal cookie, you could have a plain cookie such as a digestive or gingersnap.

You can add an extra egg white to your omelet. An egg white has no cholesterol and only 20 calories. An egg yolk has 60 calories.

Try this in your omelet:
- *a sprinkle of dried or fresh dill or parsley*
- *1 tablespoon (15 mL) of finely chopped onion, green onion or chives*

This dinner is higher in fat than usual. You can reduce the fat by cutting down or omitting the margarine on your toast.

Try these soft-textured oatmeal cookies.

Oatmeal Cookies

Makes 36 cookies

Per cookie	
Calories	78
Carbohydrate	14 g
Fiber	1 g
Protein	1 g
Fat, total	2 g
Fat, saturated	0 g
Cholesterol	5 mg
Sodium	71 mg

⅓ cup (75 mL) margarine

¾ cup (175 mL) packed brown sugar

1 egg

½ cup (125 mL) skim milk

1 tsp (5 mL) vanilla

1 cup (250 mL) flour

1 tsp (5 mL) baking powder

1 tsp (5 mL) baking soda

1 tsp (5 mL) ground cinnamon

1½ cups (375 mL) quick-cooking oats or large-flaked oats

1 cup (250 mL) raisins

1. In a large mixing bowl, mix together the margarine, brown sugar and egg. Beat with a wooden spoon until smooth. Beat in the milk and vanilla.
2. In a medium bowl, mix together the flour, baking powder, baking soda, cinnamon, and rolled oats.
3. Add the flour and oats to the large bowl. Stir well. Add the raisins and stir again.
4. Drop small spoonfuls of batter onto a nonstick baking sheet or lightly greased regular cookie sheet. Batter will be sticky. Bake in a 375°F (190°C) oven for about 10 minutes, or until golden.

To keep your nonstick pans and nonstick cookie sheets in good shape, use a plastic spatula or plastic spoon rather than a metal one. Store your nonstick pans so that other pots aren't scratching them. I wrap mine in tea towels.

Food Choices	Large Meal	Small Meal
Carbohydrate	4	3
Meat and Alternatives	3	2
Fat	2½	1½
Nutritional Info	Large Meal	Small Meal
Carbohydrate	72 g	60 g
Fiber	9 g	9 g

Your Dinner Menu	Large Meal (730 calories)	Small Meal (550 calories)
Cheese Omelet	1 large	1 small
Toast	2 slices	2 slices
Margarine	2 tsp (10 mL)	1 tsp (5 mL)
Broccoli	2 cups (500 mL) of pieces	2 cups (500 mL) of pieces
Light cheese spread	1 tbsp (15 mL)	1 tbsp (15 mL)
Oatmeal cookies	2	1

SMALL MEAL

DINNER 10

Ham & Sweet Potato

For this meal, buy a cooking ham. Look for one that has the least amount of fat. Put the ham on a rack in a roasting pan. Bake your ham for about 25 minutes per pound (1½ hours per kg) at 325°F (160°C). If you are using a thermometer, cook to 160°F (71°C).

You can flavor and decorate the top of your ham by pushing about one dozen whole cloves into the outside of the ham. I usually put slices of pineapple on top of the ham for the last 30 minutes of the cooking.

Mustard can be enjoyed with your ham.

A sweet potato has different vitamins and minerals than a regular potato, and it's nice for a change. Like orange squash and carrots, sweet potato is rich in vitamin A — important for healthy eyes. Since your oven is on, cook it like a regular baked potato. Poke it with a fork and cook until tender. Bake it for 1 hour.

Try these Seasoned Bread Crumbs sprinkled on your cauliflower. You can also sprinkle the Seasoned Bread Crumbs on other vegetables and on baked dishes.

Hams have a small amount of either sugar or honey added. "Honey" ham does not have more sugar than regular ham, but all hams contain a lot of salt.

Sweet potatoes are a powerhouse of vitamin A, which is important for good vision and healthy teeth, nails, hair, bones and glands. It also helps protect against infection and is an antioxidant (fighting cancer and heart disease). The deeper the orange color of the sweet potato, the richer the source of vitamin A. Sweet potatoes are also a good source of fiber, vitamin C and potassium.

Sweet potato can also be cooked by:
- *microwaving it at high for 10 minutes*
- *boiling it with the skin on (take off the skin, once it is cooked)*

Seasoned Bread Crumbs

Makes just over 1 cup (250 mL)

You can buy bread crumbs, or make your own by crushing dry bread and adding spices.

| 1 cup (250 mL) dry bread crumbs |
| 2 tbsp (25 mL) parmesan cheese |
| 1 tbsp (15 mL) dried parsley |
| 1 tsp (5 mL) dried oregano |
| ½ tsp (2 mL) garlic powder |
| ⅛ tsp (0.5 mL) pepper |

Per 1 tsp (5 mL)	
Calories	10
Carbohydrate	2 g
Fiber	0 g
Protein	0 g
Fat, total	0 g
Fat, saturated	0 g
Cholesterol	0 mg
Sodium	24 mg

1. Mix ingredients together. Store Seasoned Bread Crumbs in the fridge or freezer.

All vegetables are good choices but some, such as cauliflower, broccoli and yellow beans, have a higher amount of fiber and water. This makes them low in calories.

Low-calorie vegetables:

- asparagus
- green or yellow beans
- bean sprouts
- broccoli
- Brussels sprouts
- cabbage
- cauliflower
- celery
- cucumber
- eggplant
- fiddleheads
- leafy greens, such as lettuce and spinach
- marrow
- mushrooms
- okra
- onions
- green or red peppers
- radishes
- summer and spaghetti squash
- tomato
- zucchini

Whipped Gelatin

Makes 4 cups (1 L)

1 package (4-serving size) light gelatin of your favorite flavor

1. Make the gelatin according to the directions on the box (or use the recipe on page 117).
2. Remove the gelatin from the fridge after about 45 minutes. It should be as thick as an unbeaten egg white. Beat the gelatin with a beater until it is foamy and has doubled in size.
3. Put it back in the fridge until firm.

Per 1 cup (250 mL)

Calories	5
Carbohydrate	2 g
Fiber	0 g
Protein	0 g
Fat, total	0 g
Fat, saturated	0 g
Cholesterol	0 mg
Sodium	25 mg

Food Choices	Large Meal	Small Meal
Carbohydrate	5	4
Meat and Alternatives	5	3
Fat	2	1

Nutritional Info	Large Meal	Small Meal
Carbohydrate	101 g	74 g
Fiber	9 g	9 g

Your Dinner Menu	Large Meal (730 calories)	Small Meal (550 calories)
Baked ham	1 thick slice (5 oz/150 g, cooked)	1 thin slice (3 oz/90 g, cooked)
Pineapple, packed in juice	2 rings, no juice	2 rings, no juice
Sweet potato	1 large	1 medium
Margarine	2 tsp (10 mL)	1 tsp (5 mL)
Cauliflower	2 cups (500 mL)	2 cups (500 mL)
Seasoned Bread Crumbs	1 tsp (5 mL)	1 tsp (5 mL)
Skim milk or 1% milk	1 cup (250 mL)	1 cup (250 mL)
Whipped Gelatin	1 cup (250 mL)	1 cup (250 mL)

SMALL MEAL

Beef Stew

Beef stew served with potatoes and bread is an old favorite. This recipe is lower in fat, as it uses lean meat and only a small amount of added fat.

Double the recipe if you want to make more to freeze for another day.

Vegetables that go well in a stew include turnips, yellow and green beans, carrots and peas. You can use frozen mixed vegetables in this recipe in place of the fresh vegetables.

If you are in a hurry, try this:
Open a can of beef stew, put it in a pot and add some frozen or cooked vegetables. Cook until heated.

Beef Stew	Per 1 cup (250 mL)
Recipe makes 7 cups (1.75 L)	Calories 164
1 tbsp (15 mL) margarine or oil	Carbohydrate . . . . . 13 g
2 medium onions, chopped	Fiber . . . . 3 g
2 cloves garlic, chopped (or ½ tsp/2 mL garlic powder)	Protein . . . . 14 g Fat, total . . . . 6 g
1 lb (500 g) stewing beef, remove any fat and chop (cut in the size of a "dice")	Fat, saturated . . . . . . 2 g Cholesterol . . . . . 27 mg
2 tbsp (25 mL) flour	Sodium . . . . 179 mg
1 to 2 packets (4.5 g each) reduced-salt beef bouillon, mixed in 2 cups (500 mL) hot water	
1 bay leaf (remove before serving)	
2 large stalks of celery, sliced	
3 medium carrots, sliced	
2 cups (500 mL) other fresh vegetables (or frozen mixed vegetables)	
⅛ tsp (0.5 mL) pepper	
¼ cup (50 mL) dry wine (or wine vinegar)	

1. Place the margarine, onions and garlic in a heavy pot. Cook and stir on medium heat until the onions become clear. Stir often so they do not burn.
2. Add the meat and stir it until it is cooked on the outside (about 5 minutes). Sprinkle the flour over the onion and meat mixture, and stir until the flour disappears.
3. Take the pot off the heat while you add the rest of the ingredients. Stir. Return to heat. Bring to a boil and then turn the heat down to low. Cover and simmer for about an hour. Stir occasionally.
4. If you are using frozen mixed vegetables instead of fresh vegetables, add them just at the end and simmer for 10 minutes.

North African Stew and Couscous

For a change, you may want a spicier stew. Try a North African stew. This stew would commonly be made with lamb and, for vegetables, onions, carrots, turnips, tomatoes, zucchini, pumpkin and squash. When you cook the meat, add 1 teaspoon (5 mL) of each of the following: turmeric, cinnamon and cumin (or try 1 tablespoon/15 mL of curry powder, instead), and 1 teaspoon (5 mL) of chili powder. Make this stew a day ahead so that the spice taste is best.

Instead of having this stew with bread and potatoes, you can serve it with couscous. Serve 1¼ cups (300 mL) couscous for the large meal and 1 cup (250 mL) for the small meal. Couscous is made from semolina wheat and can be bought in all major food stores. It looks like rice and tastes like noodles. It is easy and quick to make because you just boil it in water. Serve the stew and couscous with mint tea.

For dessert, enjoy a serving of melon or other fruit.

Food Choices	Large Meal	Small Meal
Carbohydrate	5	4
Meat and Alternatives	3½	2½
Fat	1	½
Nutritional Info	**Large Meal**	**Small Meal**
Carbohydrate	104 g	80 g
Fiber	12 g	9 g

Your Dinner Menu	Large Meal (730 calories)	Small Meal (550 calories)
Beef Stew	2 cups (500 mL)	1½ cups (375 mL)
Boiled potatoes	1 large	1 medium
Bread	1 slice	1 slice
Margarine	1 tsp (5 mL)	½ tsp (2 mL)
Sliced cucumbers	½ medium cucumber	½ medium cucumber
Melon	2 slices	2 slices

SMALL MEAL

Fish & Chips

This is an easy meal prepared with ready-made frozen fish sticks and frozen french fries. Bake them in the oven on a cookie sheet. The portions of fish sticks and the frozen french fries are kept small because of the fat in them. This meal has a lot less fat than battered fish and french fries that are deep-fried in oil.

Look for brands of fish sticks that are labeled "low in fat." These are often made with less oil or a lighter batter.

You can also make Baked Low-Fat Fries at home using the recipe below. The photograph shows the store-bought frozen french fries, not these homemade ones.

Baked Low-Fat Fries

Makes 45 fries (15 fries for each potato)

3 medium potatoes (about 1 lb/500 g)

1 egg white

1 to 2 tsp (5 to 10 mL) packaged potato seasonings, or sprinkle on your favorite herbs or spices (such as curry, garlic powder, dill, Cajun spice or hot pepper flakes)

Per 10 fries	
Calories	65
Carbohydrate	14 g
Fiber	1 g
Protein	2 g
Fat, total	0 g
Fat, saturated	0 g
Cholesterol	0 mg
Sodium	63 mg

1. Wash and peel the potatoes.
2. Cut into fry-size pieces or chunks.
3. In a small bowl, mix the egg white and spices with a fork.
4. Dip the potato pieces into the mixture.
5. Bake the potato pieces on a greased nonstick cookie sheet at 400°F (200°C). Cook for about 30 minutes, turning them every 10 minutes.

With this meal, have one vegetable serving of squash, peas, carrots, corn, turnips or parsnips.

Here is how I cooked the squash shown in the photograph: Cut a squash in half and place the cut side down on a cookie sheet. Bake in the oven with the fish and fries. Bake for 30 minutes, or until tender.

You could have store-bought chicken nuggets with your fries and vegetables instead of fish sticks.

- *for the large meal you could have 7 chicken nuggets (4$\frac{1}{2}$ oz/140 g)*
- *for the small meal you could have 5 chicken nuggets (3$\frac{1}{4}$ oz/95 g).*

Compare the calories of 10 french fries:

- *fried in oil from a restaurant: 160 calories.*
- *frozen fries baked in the oven: 90 calories.*
- *Baked Low-Fat Fries: 60 calories.*

Squash
The orange squash shown in the photograph is an acorn squash. There are many kinds of squash. For example you may want to try spaghetti squash, one of the less sweet squashes.

Try this light Jellied Vegetable Salad. It is colorful and tasty and low in calories. The lime gelatin gives it a nice green color.

Jellied Vegetable Salad

Makes 2½ cups (625 mL)
(5 servings)

1 package (4-serving size) light lime gelatin

1½ cups (375 mL) boiling water

2 tbsp (25 mL) lemon or lime juice

½ cup (125 mL) finely chopped radish

½ cup (125 mL) finely chopped celery

½ cup (125 mL) finely chopped cabbage

1 tbsp (15 mL) chopped fresh or dried parsley

Per ½ cup (125 mL)	
Calories	17
Carbohydrate	4 g
Fiber	1 g
Protein	1 g
Fat, total	0 g
Fat, saturated	0 g
Cholesterol	0 mg
Sodium	41 mg

1. In a medium bowl, place the gelatin powder. Add the boiling water and stir until the gelatin is mixed in. Add the lemon juice. Put this mixture in the fridge.
2. Chop all the vegetables. Once the mixture in the fridge is slightly thickened (about 45 minutes), stir in all the vegetables.
3. Chill until set (about another hour).

Jellied Vegetable Salad can be a low-calorie vegetable choice with any lunch or dinner meal — ½ cup (125 mL) has only 20 calories.

For a lightly salted and less sweet flavor in the Jellied Vegetable Salad, try this:
- *add 1 packet (4.5 g) of light chicken bouillon mix, or 1 bouillon cube, to the boiling water.*

Food Choices	Large Meal	Small Meal
Carbohydrate	4	3
Meat and Alternatives	3	2
Fat	1	1
Nutritional Info	Large Meal	Small Meal
Carbohydrate	90 g	71 g
Fiber	8 g	7 g

Your Dinner Menu	Large Meal (730 calories)	Small Meal (550 calories)
Fish sticks	6 sticks or 3 wedges	4 sticks or 2 wedges
Oven-baked frozen french fries	15	10
Ketchup	1 tbsp (15 mL)	1 tbsp
Squash	½ cup (125 mL)	½ cup (125 mL)
Jellied Vegetable Salad	½ cup (125 mL)	½ cup (125 mL)
Plum	1 medium	1 medium

SMALL MEAL

DINNER 13

Zucchini is also nice cooked in a pan with 1 teaspoon (5 mL) of margarine or oil and chopped onion and garlic. To this you can add one or two other vegetables, such as:
- *canned or fresh chopped tomatoes*
- *green pepper*
- *eggplant*

Add water to the pan, if needed. Sprinkle parmesan cheese on top.

Sausages & Cornbread

Sausages are high in fat and salt, so should be eaten only occasionally. Here are the best ways to cook them to remove some of the fat. First poke them several times so the fat can drain out.
- broil on a rack, or barbecue
- boil for 10 minutes, then bake in the oven until brown
- microwave sausages on a rack

Fill up on vegetables. Zucchini is a low-calorie vegetable that is easy to prepare by slicing and steaming. If you boil zucchini, it will get soggy. Sprinkle it with Seasoned Bread Crumbs (see recipe on page 148).

Use the coleslaw recipe in Lunch 5 on page 86. You could replace the light ice cream bar with ½ cup (125 mL) skim milk.

Cornbread or Corn Muffins

Makes an 8-inch (2 L) square pan (12 pieces) or 12 muffins

	Per piece (¹/₁₂ of recipe)
¾ cup (175 mL) cornmeal	Calories 137
1¼ cups (300 mL) skim milk	Carbohydrate . . . . . 21 g
	Fiber . . . . 1 g
1 egg, slightly beaten	Protein . . . . 3 g
3 level tbsp (45 mL) oil or melted margarine, butter or shortening	Fat, total . . . . 4 g
	Fat, saturated . . . . . . 0 g
	Cholesterol . . . . . 16 mg
1 cup (250 mL) flour	Sodium . . . . 180 mg
1 tbsp (15 mL) baking powder	
½ tsp (2 mL) salt	
¼ cup (50 mL) sugar	

For a change, here are some starches that could take the place of 1 piece of cornbread:
- *½ cup (125 mL) canned corn kernels or rice*
- *1 small cob of corn*

1. In a medium bowl, mix together the cornmeal, milk, slightly beaten egg and oil (or melted fat).
2. In a large bowl, mix together the flour, baking powder, salt and sugar.
3. Add the cornmeal mixture to the flour mixture. Stir until combined. Pour into an 8-inch (2 L) square pan or muffin tin. Use a nonstick pan, or grease your pan lightly.
4. Bake in a 400°F (200°C) oven for about 20 minutes (15 minutes for muffins), or until lightly browned.
5. Cut into 12 pieces (about 3 inches by 2 inches/7.5 cm by 5 cm).

Food Choices	Large Meal	Small Meal
Carbohydrate	4	3
Meat and Alternatives	1½	1

Nutritional Info	Large Meal	Small Meal
Carbohydrate	89 g	78 g
Fiber	10 g	9 g

Your Dinner Menu	Large Meal (730 calories)	Small Meal (550 calories)
Sausages	4 small links	3 small links
Cornbread	2½ pieces	2 pieces
Steamed zucchini	2 cups (500 mL)	2 cups (500 mL)
Seasoned Bread Crumbs	1 tbsp (15 mL)	1 tbsp (15 mL)
Coleslaw	½ cup (125 mL)	½ cup (125 mL)
Light fudge ice cream bar	1 bar	1 bar

SMALL MEAL

DINNER 14

Chili Con Carne

Chili Con Carne

Makes 6¼ cups (1.55 L)

Per 1 cup (250 mL)	
Calories	270
Carbohydrate	29 g
Fiber	7 g
Protein	21 g
Fat, total	8 g
Fat, saturated	3 g
Cholesterol	38 mg
Sodium	597 mg

1 lb (500 g) lean ground beef

2 medium onions, chopped

28-oz (796 mL) can kidney beans, drained and rinsed

10-oz (284 mL) can tomato soup

1 cup (250 mL) water

⅛ tsp (0.5 mL) pepper

½ tsp (2 mL) chili powder

1 tbsp (15 mL) vinegar

½ tsp (2 mL) Worcestershire sauce

1 cup (250 mL) chopped vegetables, such as celery or green pepper

Chili freezes well. You can easily double the recipe for freezing.

All canned beans contain a lot of salt, but the sodium can be reduced by draining off the liquid they are packed in and rinsing them thoroughly before use.

Instead of ⅓ cup (75 mL) of rice:
- *1 slice of bread*
- *1 piece of bannock*
- *1 small potato*

1. In a large, heavy pot, brown the ground beef. Drain off as much fat as you can.
2. Add all the other ingredients to the pot.
3. Cover with a lid and cook for 2 to 3 hours on low heat. Stir every now and then so the chili doesn't stick. Add extra water if it gets too thick.

Serve the meal with brown or white rice.

Add a low-calorie vegetable such as yellow beans or green beans. Carrot sticks are served on the side.

For a dessert treat, try this tasty Baked Apple or have a serving of any other kind of fruit.

These baked apples have a lovely glaze because of the combination of brown sugar and butter. Margarine can be used instead, but butter makes the syrup thicker.

This recipe has less fat and sugar than a traditional baked apple. Regular sugar is used because low-calorie sweeteners tend to make the syrup in the apple too thin.

A baked apple helps satisfy a sweet tooth, and has less fat and sugar than a piece of apple pie.
- *A 3$\frac{1}{2}$-inch (8.5 cm) piece of apple pie usually has about 7 teaspoons (35 mL) of added sugar and starch and 3 teaspoons (15 mL) of added fat.*
- *One of these Baked Apples has 1$\frac{1}{2}$ teaspoons (7 mL) of added sugar and $\frac{1}{2}$ teaspoon (2 mL) of added fat.*

Baked Apple

Makes 2 baked apples

2 medium apples

1 tsp (5 mL) butter or margarine

1 tbsp (15 mL) brown sugar

$\frac{1}{4}$ tsp (1 mL) ground cinnamon

$\frac{1}{4}$ tsp (1 mL) lemon juice

Dash of nutmeg (if desired)

1 tbsp (15 mL) raisins

Per apple

Calories	141
Carbohydrate	32 g
Fiber	3 g
Protein	0 g
Fat, total	2 g
Fat, saturated	1 g
Cholesterol	5 mg
Sodium	23 mg

1. Remove apple core, cutting from the top of the apple. Don't cut right through to the bottom. Prick apples with a fork.
2. In a small bowl, mix together the other ingredients and spoon into the apples.
3. Place apples on a dish and microwave them on High for 80 seconds, or until the apples are tender. Or place the apples in a pan with 2 tablespoons (25 mL) of water and bake in a 350°F (180°C) oven for 30 minutes.

Food Choices	Large Meal	Small Meal
Carbohydrate	6	4$\frac{1}{2}$
Meat and Alternatives	4	3

Nutritional Info	Large Meal	Small Meal
Carbohydrate	120 g	91 g
Fiber	19 g	15 g

Your Dinner Menu	Large Meal (730 calories)	Small Meal (550 calories)
Chili Con Carne	1$\frac{1}{2}$ cups (375 mL)	1 cup (250 mL)
Rice	$\frac{2}{3}$ cup (150 mL)	$\frac{1}{3}$ cup (75 mL)
Green beans	1 cup (250 mL)	1 cup (250 mL)
Carrot sticks	1 medium carrot	1 medium carrot
Baked Apple	1	1

SMALL MEAL

DINNER 15

Perogies

Buy frozen perogies and enjoy a fast-food meal, at home. Perogies come with many fillings, such as cheese, potato, cottage cheese and even pizza. The starch in perogies can add up quickly, so be careful not to eat more than the number shown in the photograph.

First, fry onions at low heat in 1 to 2 teaspoons (5 to 10 mL) of fat (add water if pan gets dry). Then take the onions out of the pan so they don't get overcooked. Fry the perogies in the same pan until lightly browned. Another way to cook them is to boil them for 10 minutes.

Instead of having a 2-ounce (60 g) piece of garlic sausage (kielbasa) with the large meal, you could have:

- $\frac{1}{2}$ cup (125 mL) of 1% cottage cheese
- 1 small fast-fry pork chop (3 oz/85 g)
- 2 slices bologna, broiled or fried, without added fat

Instead of the beet soup, you may want to have 1 cup (250 mL) of cooked beets. Pickled beets have added sugar, so $\frac{1}{2}$ cup (125 mL) of these would equal 1 cup (250 mL) of beet soup.

Perogies and sour cream go together like hugs and kisses; but go for a light hug. Enjoy 1 tablespoon (15 mL) of light sour cream, or 2 tablespoons (25 mL) of fat-free sour cream with your perogies.

- *Fat-free sour cream has only 9 calories in 1 tablespoon (15 mL).*
- *Light sour cream (7% fat) has 16 calories in 1 tablespoon (15 mL).*
- *Regular sour cream (14% fat) has 32 calories in 1 tablespoon (15 mL).*

Easy Beet Soup

Makes 3½ cups (875 mL)

10-oz (284 mL) can diced beets
(unsweetened), drained and rinsed

1½ cups (375 mL) vegetable juice
(such as V8)

½ cup (125 mL) water

2 cups (500 mL) chopped cabbage

¼ tsp (1 mL) dried dill

Per 1 cup (250 mL)	
Calories	46
Carbohydrate	10 g
Fiber	2 g
Protein	2 g
Fat, total	0 g
Fat, saturated	0 g
Cholesterol	0 mg
Sodium	363 mg

1. Place all ingredients in a pot.
2. Cover and simmer. Stir as it is cooking. It will take about 15 minutes to cook.

Serve with a dab of low-fat sour cream and green onion tops.

For a low-calorie vegetable, have sauerkraut or a dill pickle. A low-salt alternative to sauerkraut or a pickle would be a small salad.

For dessert, have 1 fresh peach. If you want canned peaches, have two halves with 2 tablespoons (25 mL) of juice. Choose fruit canned in water or juice. Have 1 plain cookie with your fruit. Plain bought cookies include arrowroot biscuits, digestives, raisin cookies (as shown in the photograph), gingersnaps, oatmeal cookies and Graham wafers.

Canned vegetables are high in sodium and should be drained and rinsed before use. Adding the liquid they are packed in to your recipes will increase the amount of sodium you consume.

Food Choices	Large Meal	Small Meal
Carbohydrate	5	4
Meat and Alternatives	2	1
Fat	1	1
Nutritional Info	**Large Meal**	**Small Meal**
Carbohydrate	104 g	83 g
Fiber	14 g	12 g

Your Dinner Menu	Large Meal (730 calories)	Small Meal (550 calories)
Perogies	6	4
Low-fat or fat-free sour cream	1 tbsp (15 mL)	1 tbsp (15 mL)
Cooked sliced onion in margarine	½ small onion 1 tsp (5 mL)	½ small onion 1 tsp (5 mL)
Garlic sausage (kielbasa)	2 oz (60 g)	1 oz (30 g)
Easy Beet Soup	1 cup (250 mL)	1 cup (250 mL)
Cherry tomatoes	2, or 2 slices of tomato	2, or 2 slices of tomato
Sauerkraut	½ cup (125 mL)	½ cup (125 mL)
Peach	1 large	1 large
Plain cookie	1	1

SMALL MEAL

DINNER 16

Hamburger with Potato Salad

If you add ¹/₂ cup (125 mL) of fresh chopped mushrooms into your raw ground meat, this will keep your hamburgers moist.

Hamburger safety
Cook hamburgers until well done to make sure they are safe to eat. There must be no pink showing. Refrigerate any leftovers right away.

If you would like to have hot dogs (wiener in a bun with onion, ketchup and mustard) instead of hamburgers, you can have:
- *instead of the cheese-burger for the large meal, 2 hot dogs with no cheese.*
- *instead of a hamburger for the small meal, 1 hot dog with cheese.*

Use lean or extra-lean ground hamburger when you make hamburgers. One pound of lean hamburger will make 3 large or 4 medium cooked hamburger patties. For extra flavor, you can mix spices or 2 teaspoons (10 mL) of dried onion soup into the raw hamburger.

Here are several ways to cook your hamburgers:
- grill on a barbecue
- place them on a rack and broil in the oven
- fry them in a nonstick pan, and soak up the extra fat with a paper towel

Fill your hamburger bun with lots of lettuce, tomato and onion. Add a teaspoon (5 mL) of ketchup, mustard and relish or cheese spread, if you wish. For the large meal, add 1 slice of cheese.

Potato Salad

Makes 4 cups (1 L) of potato salad

Per ½ cup (125 mL)	
Calories	85
Carbohydrate	15 g
Fiber	1 g
Protein	2 g
Fat, total	2 g
Fat, saturated	0 g
Cholesterol	24 mg
Sodium	52 mg

4 small cooked potatoes, chopped

½ green pepper, finely chopped

2 stalks celery, finely chopped

2 to 3 green onions, finely chopped
(or 1 small onion)

5 radishes, sliced

2 tbsp (25 mL) vinegar

2 tbsp (25 mL) light mayonnaise

½ tsp (2 mL) prepared mustard

Salt and pepper, to taste

1 hard-boiled egg, chopped

Dash of paprika to sprinkle on top

1. In a big bowl, mix together the potatoes, green pepper, celery, green onions and radishes.
2. In a small bowl, mix together the vinegar, mayonnaise, mustard, salt and pepper. Gently fold in the chopped egg. Pour this into the bowl with the potatoes, and mix gently. Sprinkle the top with paprika.

A nice drink for this meal is light iced tea. There are many kinds that you can buy. You could make your own light iced tea by mixing leftover cold tea with lemon juice and a low-calorie sweetener, to suit your taste.

Watermelon or some other fresh fruit is a great end to this meal.

Potato salad safety
Once you've made your potato salad, keep it in your refrigerator. As soon as your meal is over, place it back in your refrigerator. Never leave it in the sun.

Check the label of light iced tea packages:
- *Make sure the tea you buy has fewer than 20 calories in a serving.*
- *It will probably say "diet", "calorie-reduced" or "light ("lite") on the label.*

Food Choices	Large Meal	Small Meal
Carbohydrate	4½	4
Meat and Alternatives	5	3½

Nutritional Info	Large Meal	Small Meal
Carbohydrate	78 g	68 g
Fiber	7 g	6 g

Your Dinner Menu	Large Meal (730 calories)	Small Meal (550 calories)
Cheeseburger/hamburger with bun and toppings	Large burger, with cheese	Medium burger
Potato Salad	¾ cup (175 mL)	½ cup (125 mL)
Celery sticks	2 stalks	2 stalks
Dill pickles	2 small, or 1 medium	2 small, or 1 medium
Light iced tea	12 oz (375 mL)	12 oz (375 mL)
Watermelon	3 small slices	3 small slices

SMALL MEAL

DINNER 17

Roast Turkey Dinner

Roast turkey is a great meal to have any time of the year. The leftovers come in so handy for sandwiches and other meals. I've made this meal fancier by adding some extras. Even with the extras, the calories in this meal are not any higher than the other meals.

Turkey

- Place your turkey on a rack, breast side up in a covered pan. For the last 15 minutes of cooking, uncover the pan if you wish.
- Cook your turkey for about 15 minutes per pound in a 350°F (180°C) oven. Cook to 170°F (77°C) measured with a thermometer in the inner thigh. Turkey is cooked when the meat moves easily when pierced with a fork.
- Once cooked, remove most of the high-fat skin, and slice the dark and white meat. Dark meat has more fat than white meat.
- Enjoy 1 tablespoon (15 mL) of canned or homemade cranberry sauce on the side.

Potatoes and Gravy

- Use the recipe for Low-Fat Gravy (page 124) and Low-Fat Mashed Potatoes (page 140).

Vegetables

- A lot of vegetables are served with this meal, including carrots, peas, dill pickles, Jellied Vegetable Salad (see recipe on page 157) and asparagus (fresh or canned).

Beverage

In addition to your glass of water, this meal is served with a wine spritzer. A spritzer has fewer calories and alcohol than regular wine. To make a glass of spritzer, add to a glass: 2 oz (60 mL) of dry wine, and fill up the glass with diet ginger ale or diet 7-Up.

I leave my turkey unstuffed. Bread stuffing is made with a lot of fat and soaks up more fat from the turkey. If you want to make stuffing — cook it in a greased baking dish (covered) or foil. Eat less potato if you also want stuffing.

If you decide to have regular gravy, limit yourself to 1 tablespoon (15 mL).

If you would prefer to not have alcohol:
- *use non-alcohol wine in the spritzer*
- *drink diet soft drink, sparkling mineral water or soda water*

Dessert

This crustless pumpkin pie is delicious. When I served this to my family, they didn't even miss the crust. It can be served as it is, or with a small amount of a whipped topping.

Crustless Pumpkin Pie

Makes 6 slices (9-inch/23 cm glass pie plate)

14-oz (398 mL) can pumpkin

½ cup (125 mL) sugar

½ tsp (2 mL) salt

½ tsp (2 mL) ground ginger

1 tsp (5 mL) ground cinnamon

¼ tsp (1 mL) ground nutmeg

¼ tsp (1 mL) ground cloves

2 eggs, slightly beaten

13-oz (385 mL) can evaporated skim milk

Per slice	
Calories	168
Carbohydrate	31 g
Fiber	2 g
Protein	8 g
Fat, total	2 g
Fat, saturated	1 g
Cholesterol	65 mg
Sodium	298 mg

1. In a large bowl, mix pumpkin, sugar, salt and spices.
2. Stir in the 2 slightly beaten eggs and mix well.
3. Add the evaporated skim milk (shake can before opening) and stir until smooth.
4. Pour into a lightly greased glass pie plate (this recipe works best in a glass pie plate instead of metal). Bake in a 400°F (200°C) oven for about 40 minutes, or until knife inserted near the center of the pie comes out clean.

*A*nother option for a topping would be vanilla yogurt.

*C*heck the label; whipped topping should have fewer than 20 calories in a 2-tablespoon (25 mL) serving.

*T*his pie is best if made the day before.

Food Choices	Large Meal	Small Meal
Carbohydrate	4½	3½
Meat and Alternatives	5	3

Nutritional Info	Large Meal	Small Meal
Carbohydrate	98 g	79 g
Fiber	11 g	9 g

Your Dinner Menu	Large Meal (730 calories)	Small Meal (550 calories)
Turkey	3 oz (90 g) white meat and 2 oz (60 g) of dark meat	3 oz (90 g) white meat (or 2 oz/60g white and 1 oz/30 g dark)
Cranberry sauce	1 tbsp (15 mL)	1 tbsp (15 mL)
Low-Fat Mashed Potatoes	1 cup (250 mL)	½ cup (125 mL)
Low-Fat Gravy	4 tbsp (60 mL)	2 tbsp (25 mL)
Peas and carrots	½ cup (125 mL)	½ cup (125 mL)
Asparagus	7 stalks	7 stalks
Dill pickle	1 medium	1 medium
Jellied Vegetable Salad	½ cup (125 mL)	½ cup (125 mL)
Wine spritzer	½ cup (125 mL)	½ cup (125 mL)
Crustless Pumpkin Pie	1 slice	1 slice
Low-fat whipped topping	1 tbsp (15 mL)	1 tbsp (15 mL)

SMALL MEAL

DINNER 18

Baked Macaroni & Cheese

Baked Macaroni and Cheese

Makes about 5$\frac{1}{2}$ cups (1.375 L)

2 cups (500 mL) dry macaroni	
2 tbsp (25 mL) skim milk	
2 eggs, beaten with a fork	
$\frac{1}{2}$ of a 10-oz (284 mL) can tomato soup	
$\frac{1}{2}$ cup (125 mL) loosely packed, shredded cheddar cheese	

2 tbsp (25 mL) Seasoned Bread Crumbs (see page 148) (optional)

Per 1 cup (250 mL)	
Calories	241
Carbohydrate	34 g
Fiber	2 g
Protein	11 g
Fat, total	7 g
Fat, saturated	3 g
Cholesterol	79 mg
Sodium	268 mg

1. Fill a heavy pot with water and bring to a boil. Add the macaroni and boil for 10 minutes. Drain.
2. Add the milk, then the eggs, to the macaroni and stir quickly on low heat until the eggs are cooked. Add the tomato soup and cheese and stir some more. It should be ready in 2 minutes.
3. It is ready to eat now if you want. If you want it baked (as in the picture), place it in a baking dish and sprinkle Seasoned Bread Crumbs on top. Bake in a 375°F (190°C) oven for 30 minutes.

Vegetables

- Cut broccoli in pieces and steam or lightly boil. For other low-calorie vegetable choices, see page 149.
- Try raw pieces of rutabaga or turnip. For a change, cook turnip with carrots, and mash together once cooked.

Macaroni and cheese is a high-carbohydrate dish, so an option is to add 1 cup (250 mL) of chopped leftover meat, chicken or fish to the recipe and omit the dessert.

Instead of 2 eggs, use a 6-oz (170 g) can of water-packed tuna with the water drained.

Use a low-fat cheese in this recipe and you will be eating less fat.

For extra flavor, add one of these to macaroni and cheese:
- *dash of hot pepper sauce*
- *1 tablespoon (15 mL) of salsa*
- *$\frac{1}{4}$ teaspoon (1 mL) each of oregano and garlic powder*

For dessert, try this easy and delicious dessert, made with bananas, pineapple, pudding and Graham wafers. It looks as good as it tastes.

Pineapple Surprise

Makes 6 servings

Per serving	
Calories	141
Carbohydrate	25 g
Fiber	1 g
Protein	3 g
Fat, total	4 g
Fat, saturated	3 g
Cholesterol	1 mg
Sodium	283 mg

1½ cups (375 mL) skim milk

1 package (4-serving size) light vanilla instant pudding mix

1 cup (250 mL) frozen whipped topping (regular or light), thawed

8-oz (227 mL) can crushed pineapple, drained

2 small bananas, sliced thinly

¼ cup (50 mL) Graham cracker crumbs (equal to about 4 Graham crackers)

1. Pour the skim milk into a medium bowl and add the pudding mix.
2. Beat with a whisk or an electric mixer until thickened (about 2 minutes).
3. Fold in the frozen whipped topping and pineapple until well blended.
4. Add the sliced bananas and Graham cracker crumbs to the pudding mixture. Save some bananas and crumbs for the top. If you want, you can layer the pudding mixture, bananas and crumbs.
5. Put in the fridge until ready to serve.

You may want to make Pineapple Surprise with regular pudding instead of light. By doing so, you will add an extra 2½ teaspoons (12 mL) of sugar to each serving.

Food Choices	Large Meal	Small Meal
Carbohydrate	6	5
Meat and Alternatives	1½	1
Nutritional Info	**Large Meal**	**Small Meal**
Carbohydrate	115 g	89 g
Fiber	10 g	8 g

Your Dinner Menu	Large Meal (730 calories)	Small Meal (550 calories)
Baked Macaroni & Cheese	2 cups (500 mL)	1¼ cups (300 mL)
Broccoli	1½ cups (375 mL)	1½ cups (375 mL)
Rutabaga or turnip sticks	½ cup (125 mL)	½ cup (125 mL)
Bread & butter pickles	5 slices	5 slices
Pineapple Surprise	1 serving	1 serving

SMALL MEAL

DINNER 19

Pork Chop & Applesauce

Pork does not have to be a rich meal. Trim the fat and barbecue or broil small pork chops. Or cook without fat in a nonstick pan. Pork goes nicely with boiled potatoes sprinkled with fresh or dried parsley.

A small dish of applesauce is served with the pork chop. Instead of applesauce, you could slice an apple and an onion and cook them with the pork.

For another nice change, try a lamb chop with mint sauce, instead of pork chop with applesauce.

This meal is served with an easy-to-make German Bean Salad. This salad will keep in the fridge for a week. This German Bean Salad has a tangy bite; it's not sweet at all. Try making it with a flavored vinegar, as shown in the picture at the side.

You can place a rack over a pan and broil the meat in the oven. The fat will drip into the pan.

Here are some lower-fat cuts of pork:
- *loin or tenderloin*
- *leg, inside round*

German Bean Salad

Makes 4 cups (1 L)

4 cups (1 L) fresh yellow or green beans, cooked, or two 14-oz (398 mL) cans of cut beans (drained and rinsed)

$\frac{1}{2}$ medium onion, thinly sliced

2 tbsp (25 mL) vinegar

$\frac{1}{4}$ tsp (1 mL) salt (no salt if using canned beans)

Per 1 cup (250 mL)	
Calories	40
Carbohydrate	9 g
Fiber	3 g
Protein	2 g
Fat, total	0 g
Fat, saturated	0 g
Cholesterol	0 mg
Sodium	149 mg

1. Cut the beans into 1-inch (2.5 cm) pieces and place in a salad bowl. If you are using canned beans, drain them and place them in the bowl.
2. Mix with the other ingredients.
3. Leave to stand for 30 minutes. Serve.

Tapioca pudding is easy to make and healthy. Instead of this pudding you may choose a boxed light pudding, or one of the dessert choices from the other meals, or 1 cup (250 mL) of milk with a plain cookie.

Tapioca Pudding

Makes 4 servings

Per serving	
Calories	149
Carbohydrate	28 g
Fiber	0 g
Protein	6 g
Fat, total	1 g
Fat, saturated	1 g
Cholesterol	49 mg
Sodium	79 mg

1 egg, separated

2 tbsp (25 mL) sugar

2 cups (500 mL) skim milk

3 tbsp (45 mL) quick-cooking tapioca

3 tbsp (45 mL) sugar

Dash of salt

$\frac{1}{2}$ tsp (2 mL) vanilla

1. Place the egg white in a bowl and the egg yolk in a small pot. Beat the egg white with a beater until foamy. Gradually add 2 tablespoons (25 mL) of sugar until mixture forms soft peaks.
2. In the pot, beat the yolk with a fork. Add the milk to the yolk. Stir in tapioca, then add 3 tablespoons (45 mL) of sugar and salt.
3. Cook this yolk mixture to a rolling boil, stirring. Take off heat.
4. Pour a small amount of the tapioca mixture over the beaten egg white and blend. Fold the rest of the tapioca mixture into the egg white. Cool on the counter.
5. Stir tapioca after 15 minutes. Add vanilla and chill.
6. Before serving, put 1 teaspoon (5 mL) of diet jam or a small piece of fruit on top of each serving, if you want.

Food Choices	Large Meal	Small Meal
Carbohydrate	5½	4½
Meat and Alternatives	5	3

Nutritional Info	Large Meal	Small Meal
Carbohydrate	94 g	83 g
Fiber	8 g	7 g

Your Dinner Menu	Large Meal (730 calories)	Small Meal (550 calories)
Pork chop	1 medium (5 oz/150 g, cooked)	1 small (3 oz/90 g, cooked)
Applesauce	¼ cup (60 mL)	¼ cup (60 mL)
Boiled potatoes with parsley	8 mini or 1½ medium	6 mini or 1 medium
German Bean Salad	1 cup (250 mL)	1 cup (250 mL)
Tapioca Pudding	1 serving	1 serving
Coffee	1 cup (250 mL)	1 cup (250 mL)

SMALL MEAL

Tacos

You can make tacos with a lot or a little spice. You can make tacos using the Bean and Meat Filling below, or using leftover spaghetti sauce, chili con carne or chopped turkey or meat. Tacos are a favorite with my family. Tacos are so easy and kids love to help (even if it does get a bit messy making them — and eating them). For a change, you can make burritos by using a soft flour tortilla shell instead of a hard taco shell.

You could make tacos one day and burritos the next with the rest of the Bean and Meat Filling. If you're cooking for just one or two people, you'll have some extra to freeze.

Canned refried beans have a lot of fat and are not a good choice.

Here are some low-calorie vegetables that taste good in tacos:
- *bean sprouts*
- *chopped tomatoes*
- *chopped green, red or yellow peppers*
- *hot pepper rings (pickled)*
- *shredded lettuce*
- *salsa*

Bean and Meat Filling

**Makes 5 cups (1.25 L)
(enough for 20 tacos)**

1 lb (500 g) lean ground beef

1 cup (250 mL) water

½–1 package (1 to 1½ oz/30 to 45 g) taco or burrito spice mix

28 oz (796 mL) can kidney beans or white beans, drained and rinsed

Per ¼ cup (60 mL)	
Calories	70
Carbohydrate	6 g
Fiber	2 g
Protein	6 g
Fat, total	2 g
Fat, saturated	1 g
Cholesterol	12 mg
Sodium	146 mg

1. In a medium pot, brown the hamburger. Drain off as much fat as you can.
2. Stir in the water and spice mix. Cook on medium heat for 10 minutes. Add the beans and cook for another 5 minutes. Add extra water if needed to keep moist.

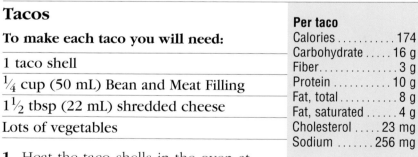

Tacos

To make each taco you will need:

1 taco shell

¼ cup (50 mL) Bean and Meat Filling

1½ tbsp (22 mL) shredded cheese

Lots of vegetables

Per taco	
Calories	174
Carbohydrate	16 g
Fiber	3 g
Protein	10 g
Fat, total	8 g
Fat, saturated	4 g
Cholesterol	23 mg
Sodium	256 mg

1. Heat the taco shells in the oven at 350°F (180°C) for 5 minutes.
2. Into each hot taco shell, put the meat and bean mixture, cheese and vegetables.

Since you eat burritos or tacos with your hands, it's nice to serve other finger foods, too. Try fresh vegetables with this dip.

Vegetable Dip

Makes 1½ cups (375 mL)

1 cup (250 mL) plain skim milk yogurt

½ cup (125 mL) low-fat sour cream

2 tbsp (25 mL) dried onion soup mix

Chopped green onion tops or parsley

Per 2 tbsp (25 mL)
Calories 26
Carbohydrate . . . . . . 4 g
Fiber. . . . . 0 g
Protein . . . . 1 g
Fat, total . . . . 1 g
Fat, saturated . . . . . . 0 g
Cholesterol . . . . . . 3 mg
Sodium . . . . 152 mg

1. Mix the first three ingredients together.
2. Put the green onions or parsley on top.

If you are looking for a low-salt vegetable dip, try this alternative recipe, which has similar calories. It has a tangy, sweet taste and is sure to be popular.

Garlic Vegetable Dip

Makes ¼ cup (50 mL).

¼ cup (50 mL) fat-free sour cream

1 tsp (5 mL) fat-free mayonnaise

1 tsp (5 mL) white vinegar

⅛ tsp (0.5 mL) no-salt-added garlic and herb seasoning, or garlic powder

½ tsp (2 mL) low-calorie sweetener (1 package)

Per 2 tbsp (25 mL)
Calories 28
Carbohydrate . . . . . . 6 g
Fiber. . . . . 0 g
Protein . . . . 1 g
Fat, total . . . . 0 g
Fat, saturated . . . . . . 0 g
Cholesterol . . . . . . 0 mg
Sodium. . . . . 66 mg

1. Combine all ingredients.

For dessert, make an angel food cake from a mix, or even easier, buy one from a bakery. Angel food cake has the lowest amount of fat of any cake. Serve the angel food cake with fruit, such as strawberries (either fresh or unsweetened frozen), and a dab of frozen or canned whipped topping. Other topping choices are listed on page 177.

Food Choices	Large Meal	Small Meal
Carbohydrate	4	3
Meat and Alternatives	2½	2

Nutritional Info	Large Meal	Small Meal
Carbohydrate	84 g	70 g
Fiber	13 g	10 g

Your Dinner Menu	Large Meal (730 calories)	Small Meal (550 calories)
Bean & Meat Tacos	3	2
Fresh vegetables on the side	2 cups (500 mL)	2 cups (500 mL)
Garlic Vegetable Dip	2 tbsp (25 mL)	2 tbsp (25 mL)
Angel food cake	¹⁄₁₀ of a 10-inch (25 cm) cake	¹⁄₁₀ of a 10-inch (25 cm) cake
Strawberries	½ cup (125 mL)	½ cup (125 mL)
Whipped topping	1 tbsp (15 mL)	1 tbsp (15 mL)

SMALL MEAL

DINNER 21

Liver & Onions

Do you love liver? Then you'll enjoy this meal. Organ meats such as liver, kidney, gizzards and heart are all rich in iron and other nutrients. But they are also high in cholesterol, so eat small servings, as shown.

Calf liver is the tastiest and most tender, but it costs more than beef liver. Pork liver is a bit stronger-tasting than beef liver.

Chicken liver is cheap, tender and tasty. Six chicken livers are equal to about one large serving of beef liver.

You can cook an equal portion of beef kidney as a change from beef liver.

Boil chicken gizzards in a bit of chicken broth for at least an hour until they are tender. About 5 ounces (140 g) raw chicken gizzards would be an equal portion to the large serving of beef liver.

Iron is needed for healthy blood. Organ meats are one of the best sources of iron. Other good sources of iron include beef, pork and chicken, eggs, oysters, kidney beans, whole wheat bread, cereals, spinach, dark green lettuce and dried fruit such as raisins.

Liver and Onions

Makes 3 large or 4 small servings

½ cup (125 mL) beef broth made from
½ cup (125 mL) water plus ½ packet
(2 g) reduced-salt beef bouillon mix

¼ cup (50 mL) dry wine or wine vinegar

4 small to medium onions, thinly sliced

1 lb (500 g) beef liver

Per small serving	
Calories	181
Carbohydrate	10 g
Fiber	2 g
Protein	24 g
Fat, total	4 g
Fat, saturated	1 g
Cholesterol	329 mg
Sodium	130 mg

1. Heat up the beef broth and wine in a nonstick or cast-iron pan. Over low heat, cook the onion slices until soft. Take the onions out of the pan, leaving the liquid.
2. Place the liver in the pan and cook it on high heat for a few minutes on each side. Make sure it is cooked through but not overcooked. Overcooking makes liver tough. Just before serving, return the onions to the pan to warm them up.
3. At the table, pour the broth from the pan over your liver and rice, if desired.

Liver is also easy and tasty cooked on the barbecue. On a hot barbecue the liver will cook quickly — be careful it doesn't overcook.

For your starch, you may have rice, as shown, or potatoes.

The vegetables for this meal are carrots and tomatoes. Choose either canned tomatoes or fresh sliced tomatoes.

For dessert, there is fruit salad served with 2 small vanilla wafers (or 1 plain cookie, such as an arrowroot biscuit). To make your fruit salad, mix together any of your favorite fresh or frozen fruits.

One cup (250 mL) of potatoes has less carbohydrate than 1 cup of rice.

Food Choices	Large Meal	Small Meal
Carbohydrate	5½	3½
Meat and Alternatives	4	3
Nutritional Info	**Large Meal**	**Small Meal**
Carbohydrate	120 g	88 g
Fiber	12 g	10 g

Your Dinner Menu	Large Meal (730 calories)	Small Meal (550 calories)
Liver and Onions	1 large serving	1 small serving
Rice	1⅓ cups (325 mL)	⅔ cup (150 mL)
Carrots	½ cup (125 mL)	½ cup (125 mL)
Canned tomatoes	1 cup (250 mL)	1 cup (250 mL)
Fresh fruit salad	1 cup (250 mL)	1 cup (250 mL)
Vanilla wafers	2 small	2 small

SMALL MEAL

DINNER 22

Sun Burger

These meatless burgers are delicious when served on a bagel or hamburger bun. Add to your bagel: lots of vegetables, such as lettuce, tomatoes, onions and cucumbers.

Bagels come in many sizes, and some are very large. A 3-inch (7.5 cm) bagel (used in this meal) is equivalent to 2 slices of bread. A 4 1/2-inch (11 cm) bagel is equivalent to 4 slices.

Bagels are quite a heavy bread. For a lower-carb option, you could choose a small whole-grain bun instead of a bagel.

Using a low-fat cheese will reduce the fat.

Sun Burgers

Makes 12 burgers

Per burger patty	
Calories	143
Carbohydrate	15 g
Fiber	4 g
Protein	8 g
Fat, total	6 g
Fat, saturated	2 g
Cholesterol	22 mg
Sodium	113 mg

1½ cups (375 mL) cooked rice, brown or white

19-oz (540 mL) can romano beans, drained (or other beans, such as pinto or kidney)

⅓ cup (75 mL) sesame seeds

⅓ cup (75 mL) sunflower seeds

2 tbsp (25 mL) wheat germ or ground flaxseed

¼ tsp (1 mL) dried basil

¼ tsp (1 mL) pepper

½ tsp (2 mL) garlic powder

1 tsp (5 mL) dried parsley

1 tsp (5 mL) of dried dillweed

1 to 2 eggs

1 cup (250 mL) loosely packed, shredded part-skim mozzarella cheese

1. Cook rice or use cold rice from the night before.
2. In a large bowl, put drained beans and mash them with a fork or a masher.
3. Add all the other ingredients. Mix with a large spoon or fork, or use your hands.
4. Form mixture into patties. Cook until nicely browned in a nonstick frying pan or heavy frying pan (lightly greased).

Add a shake of dried dill to the mayonnaise you spread on your burger.

Kale and Orange Salad

Makes 1 serving

Per serving	
Calories	64
Carbohydrate	14 g
Fiber	4 g
Protein	3 g
Fat, total	1 g
Fat, saturated	0 g
Cholesterol	0 mg
Sodium	47 mg

$\frac{3}{4}$ cup (175 mL) chopped stemmed kale leaves (chopped into fine strips)

$\frac{1}{3}$ cup (75 mL) sliced bok choy

$\frac{1}{3}$ cup (75 mL) chopped broccoli

$\frac{1}{4}$ orange, broken into segments

3 strawberries, sliced

Sprinkle of sesame seeds, ground flaxseed or walnuts (optional)

1. Combine all ingredients.
2. Add your favorite light salad dressing.

This dessert is easy to make and has a nice light flavor.

Dream Delight

Makes four 1-cup (250 mL) servings

Per cup (250 mL)	
Calories	73
Carbohydrate	8 g
Fiber	0 g
Protein	2 g
Fat, total	4 g
Fat, saturated	4 g
Cholesterol	0 mg
Sodium	43 mg

1 package (4-serving size) unflavored gelatin

1 package (4-serving size) light gelatin, raspberry or any other flavor

1$\frac{1}{4}$ cups (300 mL) boiling water

1$\frac{1}{4}$ cups (300 mL) cold water

1 package dessert topping mix (enough to make 2 cups/500 mL)

1. Place the unflavored gelatin and the light gelatin in a bowl.
2. Stir in boiling water until the gelatin is mixed in. Then stir in cold water. Refrigerate.
3. Remove the gelatin from the fridge after about 45 minutes. It should be as thick as an unbeaten egg white. Do not allow it to get too firm.
4. Mix the topping mix as directed on the box.
5. Blend topping with a beater into gelatin mixture until well mixed.
6. Pour into four dessert bowls. Refrigerate to set.

You may want to make this dessert with regular gelatin instead of light. By doing so, you will add an extra 4 teaspoons (20 mL) of sugar to each serving.

Food Choices	Large Meal	Small Meal
Carbohydrate	4	3
Meat and Alternatives	2	1
Fat	2	2

Nutritional Info	Large Meal	Small Meal
Carbohydrate	89 g	74 g
Fiber	13 g	9 g

Your Dinner Menu	Large Meal (730 calories)	Small Meal (550 calories)
Sun Burgers	2	1
Bagel	1 (3-inch/7.5 cm)	1 (3-inch/7.5 cm)
Light mayonnaise	1 tbsp (15 mL)	1 tbsp (15 mL)
Kale and Orange Salad	1 serving	1 serving
Citrus Vinaigrette (page 137)	2 tbsp (25 mL)	2 tbsp (25 mL)
Dream Delight	1 cup (250 mL)	1 cup (250 mL)

SMALL MEAL

Salmon & Potato Dish

This is one of the meals that my husband likes to make. It is easy and is always popular. It can be made with canned salmon or tuna, or any kind of leftover fish.

Add one of these to your salmon for some extra flavor:
- *$\frac{1}{2}$ teaspoon (2 mL) horseradish*
- *$\frac{1}{4}$ teaspoon (1 mL) mustard*
- *1 tablespoon (15 mL) salsa*
- *1 tablespoon (15 mL) spaghetti sauce*

Instant mashed potatoes can be used. They are softer and moister than fresh mashed potatoes.

No-salt-added canned salmon contains about 85% less sodium than the regular variety. If it's available, you can use it in Salmon and Potato Dish to reduce the sodium per serving to about 400 mg.

Salmon and Potato Dish

**Makes one small baking dish
(2 large or 3 small servings)**

1 can (7$\frac{1}{2}$ oz/213 g) pink or red salmon, drained
Pinch of pepper
1 cup (250 mL) loosely packed, shredded cheddar cheese
2 cups (500 mL) mashed potato (leftover or fresh)

Per large serving	
Calories	519
Carbohydrate	39 g
Fiber	3 g
Protein	39 g
Fat, total	23 g
Fat, saturated	13 g
Cholesterol	133 mg
Sodium	731 mg

1. Mash the salmon with the bones. Put the salmon on the bottom of a small baking dish. Sprinkle with pepper and half the shredded cheese.
2. Spread the mashed potato on top of the salmon and cheese.
3. Sprinkle the rest of the cheese on top.
4. Bake in a 350°F (180°C) oven for 30 minutes, or microwave for 8 minutes.

For a change, this dish can also be made into patties and fried in a nonstick pan.

Corn is the sweet vegetable with this meal, and spinach and tomato juice are the low-calorie vegetables.

You can buy spinach fresh or frozen.

Choose either $\frac{1}{3}$ cup (75 mL) of creamed corn or $\frac{1}{2}$ cup (125 mL) of corn kernels for your vegetable. Creamed corn has sugar added, so a smaller serving is enough.

The dessert is light gelatin with fruit.

Light Gelatin with Fruit

Makes three 1-cup (250 mL) servings

Ingredients	Per 1 cup (250 mL)
1 package (4-serving size) light gelatin	Calories 68
1 cup (250 mL) boiling water	Carbohydrate . . . . . 18 g
	Fiber . . . . 1 g
$\frac{1}{4}$ cup (50 mL) cold water	Protein . . . . 1 g
	Fat, total . . . . 0 g
14-oz (398 mL) can fruit cocktail, with juice	Fat, saturated . . . . . . 0 g
	Cholesterol . . . . . . 0 mg
	Sodium . . . . 37 mg

1. Put the gelatin in a medium bowl (not plastic).
2. Add the boiling water. Stir until gelatin is all mixed in.
3. Add the cold water and fruit cocktail and stir.
4. Pour into three dessert bowls. Refrigerate to set.

Spinach is rich in iron and folic acid.

Instead of fruit cocktail, you can use a can of other fruit, such as peaches. Chop the fruit into pieces.

If you want, you can use $1\frac{3}{4}$ cups (425 mL) of fresh chopped fruit instead of canned fruit. When you use fresh fruit, add 1 cup (250 mL) of cold water instead of $\frac{1}{4}$ cup (50 mL).

Sliced tomato would be a lower-sodium option than tomato juice. However, tomato juice is higher in lycopenes, an important antioxidant that is released from tomatoes when they are cooked. Try to buy reduced-sodium tomato juice.

Food Choices	Large Meal	Small Meal
Carbohydrate	5	$3\frac{1}{2}$
Meat and Alternatives	$4\frac{1}{2}$	3

Nutritional Info	Large Meal	Small Meal
Carbohydrate	91 g	72 g
Fiber	10 g	9 g

Your Dinner Menu	Large Meal (730 calories)	Small Meal (550 calories)
Salmon & Potato Dish	$\frac{1}{2}$ the recipe	$\frac{1}{3}$ the recipe
Corn	$\frac{3}{4}$ cup (175 mL)	$\frac{1}{2}$ cup (125 mL)
Spinach	$\frac{1}{2}$ cup (125 mL)	$\frac{1}{2}$ cup (125 mL)
Tomato juice	$\frac{1}{2}$ cup (125 mL)	$\frac{1}{2}$ cup (125 mL)
Celery	$\frac{1}{4}$ stalk (in tomato juice)	$1\frac{1}{4}$ stalks
Light Gelatin with Fruit	1 cup (250 mL)	1 cup (250 mL)

SMALL MEAL

Hamburger Noodle Dish

Most packages of noodles and sauce mix that can be added to help hamburger are high in fat. This recipe is lower in fat.

Regular canned condensed soups contain a lot of salt, but many now come in reduced-salt versions, so choose them when you can.

The mushrooms add a nice flavor to this recipe.

If you want a bit more zip, you can always add a dash of hot pepper sauce.

The corkscrew noodles look nice in this dish, but if you don't have them, use macaroni.

Hamburger Noodle Dish

Makes 7$\frac{1}{3}$ cups (1.825 L)
(about 4 large or 6 small servings)

Per 1 cup (250 mL)	
Calories	293
Carbohydrate	38 g
Fiber	3 g
Protein	18 g
Fat, total	7 g
Fat, saturated	3 g
Cholesterol	33 mg
Sodium	382 mg

1 lb (500 g) lean ground beef

1 large onion, chopped

$\frac{1}{4}$ tsp (1 mL) pepper

10-oz (284 mL) can tomato soup

10-oz (284 mL) can mushroom pieces (drained)

1 cup (250 mL) skim milk

1 tsp (5 mL) Worcestershire sauce

4 cups (1 L) dry corkscrew noodles (or 2$\frac{1}{2}$ cups/625 mL dry macaroni)

1. In a large, heavy pan, brown the hamburger. Drain off the fat.
2. Add the chopped onion to the hamburger and cook until the onions are soft. Add water if too dry. Add all other ingredients except the noodles. Cook for 15 minutes.
3. While the hamburger and onions are cooking, add the noodles to a pot of boiling water and cook as directed on package. Drain the cooked noodles.
4. Add cooked noodles to the hamburger mixture. Cook for 5 more minutes.

This meal is served with mixed vegetables and steamed cabbage. You may drizzle 1 tablespoon (15 mL) of light cheese spread on your cabbage, instead of the butter or margarine.

For dessert, have a piece of fresh fruit.

"Healthy meals and snacks give me the energy I need to do my work."

You could substitute 1 large banana for the 1 cup (250 mL) of grapes in this meal.

Food Choices	Large Meal	Small Meal
Carbohydrate	5	4
Meat and Alternatives	2½	1½
Fat	1	½

Nutritional Info	Large Meal	Small Meal
Carbohydrate	110 g	85 g
Fiber	14 g	11 g

Your Dinner Menu	Large Meal (730 calories)	Small Meal (550 calories)
Hamburger Noodle Dish	1½ cups (375 mL)	1 cup (250 mL)
Mixed vegetables	¾ cup (175 mL)	½ cup (125 mL)
Cabbage	1 cup (250 mL)	1 cup (250 mL)
Margarine or butter	1 tsp (5 mL)	½ tsp (2 mL)
Grapes	1 cup (250 mL)	1 cup (250 mL)

SMALL MEAL

Pizza

This meal can be eaten out in a restaurant or you can make the meal at home using the recipe below. The photograph shows a thick crust pizza. You may want to choose a thin crust pizza which will have less calories. Choose a pizza with lots of vegetables and don't go heavy on the meat and cheese.

If you are making your own pizza at home, you can make it lower in fat by using lean meat and low-fat cheese, and lots of vegetables of your choice. Try this easy recipe.

You can make mini pizzas on opened hamburger buns or on English muffins or pita shells.

Pizza has lots of salt because of the cheese and processed meats on top. To make a lower-sodium pizza, you could add a shredded or chopped unsalted cooked meat such as chicken (try it coated in cilantro to enhance the flavor) instead of processed meat.

When buying tomato sauce, remember to check the amount of sodium on the Nutrition Facts label. It varies a lot between brands. Look for one that has less than 400 mg of sodium per ½ cup (125 mL).

Homemade Pizza

**Makes one 12-inch (30 cm) pizza
(6 large or 8 medium slices)**

Pizza shell (ready-made, 12-inch/30 cm)

½ cup (125 mL) Pizza Sauce (see below)

Vegetables, such as mushrooms, peppers, onions, tomatoes, broccoli, zucchini, or eggplant

¾ cup (175 mL) pineapple chunks

2 oz (60 g) sliced ham, sausage or pepperoni

1 cup (250 mL) loosely packed part-skim shredded cheese

Per large slice (⅙ of pizza)	
Calories	293
Carbohydrate	41 g
Fiber	3 g
Protein	13 g
Fat, total	9 g
Fat, saturated	4 g
Cholesterol	18 mg
Sodium	570 mg

1. Spread the pizza sauce on the pizza shell.
2. Add the vegetables, pineapple and meat. Top with cheese.
3. Place on your oven rack or use a pizza pan, if you have one. Bake in a 350°F (180°C) oven for 15 minutes, until the cheese bubbles.

Pizza Sauce

Makes about 1⅔ cups (400 mL)

14-oz (398 mL) can tomato sauce

½ tsp (2 mL) oregano

½ tsp (2 mL) garlic powder or
1 garlic clove, finely chopped

Any of the following are optional for extra flavoring: 1 finely chopped small onion, ½ stalk finely chopped celery or a pinch of cinnamon or cloves

Per 2 tbsp (25 mL)	
Calories	10
Carbohydrate	2 g
Fiber	0 g
Protein	0 g
Fat, total	0 g
Fat, saturated	0 g
Cholesterol	0 mg
Sodium	157 mg

1. Combine all ingredients.

Have a salad with your pizza. Use a store-bought oil-free salad dressing or, for less sodium, try Citrus Vinaigrette (page 137). With your meal enjoy a diet soft drink (as shown) or a small glass of tomato juice. Also have water to drink.

Have a fruit for dessert.

A few restaurant tips:

- Eat a fruit or a fresh vegetable snack before you go to a restaurant so you won't be so hungry and overeat.
- It may help if you decide what you'll order before you go. Or better still, decide what you won't order.
- Start with a salad, clear soup or vegetable soup. Even fast-food restaurants now have salads.
- Ask for low-fat salad dressings on the side.
- Don't be shy about asking for foods to be made to your liking. For example, if you order a sandwich, ask for it to be unbuttered.
- If your meal is bigger than your portions should be, ask the waiter to package your leftovers so you can take them home.

Drinking regular soft drinks, sweetened beverages and even juices will give you extra sugar you don't need. Remember, water is what your body needs when you are thirsty (see page 21). For more information about sugar in beverages, go to Dinner 35.

Food Choices	Large Meal	Small Meal
Carbohydrate	5	4
Meat and Alternatives	2	1½

Nutritional Info	Large Meal	Small Meal
Carbohydrate	111 g	91 g
Fiber	9 g	7 g

Your Dinner Menu	Large Meal (730 calories)	Small Meal (550 calories)
12-inch (30 cm) Pizza	2 large slices (⅓ pizza)	2 medium slices (¼ pizza)
Tossed salad	Large	Large
Oil-free salad dressing	1 tbsp (15 mL)	1 tbsp (15 mL)
Diet soft drink	Large	Large
Nectarine	1 large	1 large

SMALL MEAL

DINNER 26

Grilled Chicken Bun & Fries

Yes, you may still eat out at fast-food restaurants — occasionally. Most foods in restaurants are high in fat and the portions are too often large or super-sized.
Since fries are the most common food ordered in restaurants, they are included in this meal; but choose a small order.

If you decide to make this meal at home, make Baked Low-Fat Fries (page 156), baked frozen french fries or a baked potato.

Instead of a grilled chicken breast on a bun (as shown in the photograph), you could order:
- a small serving of 6 chicken nuggets with sauce
- a single fish burger
- a cheeseburger

Size and ingredients at fast-food restaurants change. So ask for a nutrition information fact sheet at restaurants where you go — and order according to calorie levels.

Salad with a light dressing is included with this meal. No salad dressing is included with the small meal due to the calories (see side bar). In a restaurant, the best choice is to have your salad plain or with half a package of "light" vinegar-based dressing (vinaigrette).

Since this meal is higher in fat than other meals, a dessert is not included with the small meal.

Have water and a diet soft drink, if you like.

Try to enjoy your coffee or tea with no milk or sugar, or less of both.

Salad dressings
- *Some of the "light" salad dressings in restaurants are still high in calories. They can have up to 60 calories in one package. Check the label.*
- *The regular salad dressings in restaurants may have 200 calories in one package.*
- *Most restaurant salad dressings are also high in salt.*

Your Dinner Menu	Large Meal (730 calories)	Small Meal (550 calories)
Grilled chicken on a bun	1	1
French fries	1 small order	1 small order
Ketchup	1 tbsp (15 mL)	1 tbsp (15 mL)
Salad	1 small	1 small
Light vinaigrette salad dressing	1 package	–
Diet soft drink	Large	Large
Yogurt cone	1 small	–

SMALL MEAL

DINNER 27

Chinese Stir-Fry

Chinese Stir-Fry

Makes 4 cups (1 L)
(2 large meal servings)

Per 1 cup (250 mL)	
Calories	120
Carbohydrate	16 g
Fiber	3 g
Protein	12 g
Fat, total	2 g
Fat, saturated	0 g
Cholesterol	18 mg
Sodium	293 mg

1 small onion

1 to 2 cloves garlic, chopped

4 to 6 cups (1 to 1.5 L) loosely packed vegetable pieces

¾ cup/175 mL (or 6 oz/175 g) raw lean red meat, chicken or fish, thinly sliced

1 packet (4.5 g) reduced-salt chicken or beef bouillon mix

2 tbsp (25 mL) water

2 tsp (10 mL) cornstarch

¼ cup (50 mL) cold water

1 tbsp (15 mL) reduced-sodium soy sauce

¼ tsp (1 mL) ground ginger

*P*ut your rice on to cook before you start making the stir-fry.

Other protein choices
Instead of raw meat, chicken, or fish, you could use:

- *5 ounces (150 g) of leftover cooked chicken, meat or fish*
- *7 ounces (210 g) of shrimp (23 jumbo shrimp)*
- *½ cup (125 mL) firm tofu (cut in chunks)*
- *28 almonds*

*W*ash your knife and cutting board with hot soapy water if you use raw chicken or raw meat.

*I*f you are making Chinese food at home, use little or no fat in a pot, or a nonstick pan or wok. Your pan has to be large enough to hold all the vegetables.

1. Chop up or slice your onion, garlic and 4 cups (1 L) of vegetables. I usually put in one bowl the vegetables that need the most cooking, such as carrots and broccoli. In a second bowl I put the vegetables that need less cooking, such as bean sprouts. Put the bowls of vegetables to the side.
2. Place the raw meat (or other protein choice) in your cold wok or frying pan. Sprinkle the bouillon mix on your meat and stir. Add 2 tablespoons (25 mL) of water. Heat up your wok or frying pan and cook for about 3 minutes. If you are using cooked leftover meat instead of raw meat, it doesn't need to be cooked first.
3. Add the onions, garlic and first bowl of vegetables. Stir at high heat for 5 to 10 minutes, until cooked. Now add the second bowl of vegetables.
4. In a small bowl, mix together the cornstarch, ¼ cup (50 mL) of cold water, soy sauce and ginger. Add this to your wok. Cook for another minute or two.

When choosing rice to serve with your stir-fry, keep in mind that brown rice and parboiled (converted) rice are better choices than white rice.

Fresh vegetables are best in a stir-fry, but you could also use frozen or canned vegetables. Try any of these vegetables:

- bamboo shoots (canned)
- bean sprouts
- broccoli (pieces)
- cabbage (shredded)
- carrots or celery (sliced)
- cauliflower (pieces)
- baby corn (canned)
- mushrooms (sliced)
- green onions (chopped)
- frozen peas or whole fresh snow peas
- green pepper (strips)

This meal includes beef broth and soda crackers. To reduce salt, use just $\frac{1}{2}$ packet of bouillon, or if using canned bouillon, add half as water.

Fill up on the low-calorie vegetable dishes. You may add a bit of soy sauce to your rice if you wish. Fried rice is high in fat. In a restaurant, just mix in a bit of fried rice with your white rice, if you wish.

Stay away from deep-fried, battered foods and foods in sweet sauces.

For dessert, a fortune cookie is a good low-calorie choice. Good luck!

Food Choices	Large Meal	Small Meal
Carbohydrate	6	$4\frac{1}{2}$
Meat and Alternatives	$2\frac{1}{2}$	2
Nutritional Info	Large Meal	Small Meal
Carbohydrate	128 g	99 g
Fiber	12 g	10 g

Your Dinner Menu	Large Meal (730 calories)	Small Meal (550 calories)
Chinese Stir-Fry	2 cups (500 mL)	$1\frac{1}{2}$ cups (375 mL)
White or brown rice	1 cup (250 mL)	$\frac{2}{3}$ cup (150 mL)
Skim or 1% milk	1 cup (250 mL)	1 cup (250 mL)
Pear	1 medium	1 medium
Fortune cookies	2	1
Tea	1 cup (250 mL)	1 cup (250 mL)

SOLUTIONS WILL COME TO YOU
WHILE YOU ARE WALKING.

SMALL MEAL

DINNER 28

Denver Sandwich & Soup

To reduce the salt in the Denver Sandwich, look for low-sodium bacon. Back bacon or turkey bacon would be a lower-fat option than regular bacon.

A sandwich and soup is a light choice for dinner in a restaurant. The sandwich could be a Denver, a Western, a clubhouse or a bacon, lettuce and tomato sandwich. Ask for your bread or toast without butter or mayonnaise, or ask the waiter to "go light" on the butter or mayonnaise. Also ask the waiter to hold the french fries. If you want to make a Denver sandwich at home, here's the recipe.

Denver Sandwich

Makes 1 sandwich

	Per sandwich	
1 slice bacon or 1 oz (30 g) ham	Calories 363	
2 eggs	Carbohydrate . . . . . 27 g	
	Fiber. . . . . 4 g	
1 tbsp (15 mL) chopped parsley, green onion tops, onion or chives	Protein . . . . 21 g	
	Fat, total. . . . . 20 g	
Pepper to taste	Fat, saturated . . . . . . 5 g	
	Cholesterol . . . . 381 mg	
	Sodium . . . . 661 mg	

2 slices toast, each spread with $\frac{1}{2}$ tsp (2 mL) margarine or butter, or 1 tsp (5 mL) light mayonnaise

Lettuce

1. Chop the bacon and cook. Drain all fat and soak up extra fat with a paper towel. If you are using chopped ham instead of bacon, you don't need to cook it first.
2. In a small bowl, beat the eggs with a fork. Add the bacon or ham and the parsley or onion tops.
3. Cook in a nonstick pan free of fat. Stir on and off.
4. Place egg mix on piece of toast.
5. Add lettuce or other vegetables to the sandwich.

If you don't care for tomato soup, have vegetable soup or a glass of tomato juice instead. Mushroom and green pea soup have the most calories of all the cream soups. Choose these less often.

These cracker servings have about the same calories:
- 1 bread stick
- 2 soda crackers
- 1 snackbread cracker
- 2 melba toasts
- 1 Ritz-type party cracker

There is no dessert with this meal. If you would like to have a small fruit, then omit the bread sticks. Or choose a very low-calorie dessert such as light gelatin or a bought sugar-free popsicle.

Regular canned soups contain a lot of salt, but we're seeing more reduced-salt versions on the market, so choose them when you can. For example, 1 cup (250 mL) canned condensed tomato soup prepared with water has about 700 mg sodium; a typical lower-salt version has only 450 mg per cup.

Walking after a meal makes you feel better and helps to bring down your blood sugar
Your blood sugar goes up after a meal, and a short walk about an hour or so after eating will help you bring it down. If you can manage a half-hour or full-hour walk, this is best, but even a shorter walk of ten to fifteen minutes can help bring down your blood sugar and blood pressure after you've eaten.

Food Choices	Large Meal	Small Meal
Carbohydrate	4½	3½
Meat and Alternatives	3	2
Fat	3	2
Nutritional Info	**Large Meal**	**Small Meal**
Carbohydrate	74 g	60 g
Fiber	8 g	6 g

Your Dinner Menu	Large Meal (730 calories)	Small Meal (550 calories)
Tomato soup (made with water)	1 cup (250 mL)	1 cup (250 mL)
Bread sticks	1½	1½
Denver Sandwich	1½ sandwiches	1 sandwich
Salad	Large	Large
Fat-free ranch salad dressing	1 tbsp (15 mL)	1 tbsp (15 mL)

SMALL MEAL

Shish Kebabs

Shish kebabs can be one of the lowest-fat meal choices in a Greek or Middle Eastern restaurant. Try this delicious low-fat marinade for your meat, or simply baste your meat with your favorite barbecue sauce.

A *true Greek shish kebab is called souvlaki and is made only with meat. It would usually be soaked in olive oil, so would be high in calories.*

Shish Kebab Marinade

Makes enough for 2 shish kebabs

1–2 tbsp (25 mL) reduced-sodium soy sauce

2 tbsp (25 mL) finely chopped onion

1 clove garlic, crushed or finely chopped (or ½ tsp/2 mL garlic powder)

1 tbsp (15 mL) minced gingerroot (or 1 tsp/5 mL ground ginger)

2 tbsp (25 mL) dry wine (or wine vinegar)

Per 1 tbsp (15 mL)	
Calories	9
Carbohydrate	1 g
Fiber	0 g
Protein	0 g
Fat, total	0 g
Fat, saturated	0 g
Cholesterol	0 mg
Sodium	100 mg

1. Mix the marinade ingredients together in a dish. Place the meat in the marinade and let it sit in the fridge for a couple of hours.

Shish Kebabs

To make each shish kebab you will need:
Meat (1½-inch/4 cm cubes of lean lamb or beef)
For large meal: 4 cubes (6 oz/175 g, raw)
For small meal: 3 cubes (4 oz/125 g, raw)
Vegetables
Cherry tomatoes, whole fresh mushrooms, cubes of green pepper, whole small onions (or chunks of onion), zucchini, eggplant, or any other vegetables you like.

1. Put the meat and vegetables on skewers, as shown in the picture. Brush with the marinade. If you want your meat well done, broil or barbecue it for 5 minutes before adding the vegetables.
2. Broil or barbecue for 5 to 10 minutes or until cooked.

This Greek Salad includes tomatoes, onions, green pepper, feta cheese and black olives. Feel free to add lettuce also.

Greek Salad

Makes 2 servings

Per serving	
Calories	201
Carbohydrate	16 g
Fiber	4 g
Protein	5 g
Fat, total	14 g
Fat, saturated	4 g
Cholesterol	17 mg
Sodium	474 mg

2 large tomatoes, cut in wedges

½ medium onion, sliced

½ green pepper, in chunks

½ small cucumber

¼ cup (50 mL) feta cheese, crumbled or chunks

12 small black olives (or 4 large)

1 tbsp (15 mL) olive oil

1 tbsp (15 mL) wine vinegar

1 tsp (5 mL) oregano

1. Mix together the tomatoes, onions, green pepper, cucumber, feta cheese and olives.
2. In a small bowl, whisk together oil, vinegar and oregano. Pour over salad and toss to coat.

For a change, you can add 1 tbsp (15 mL) tomato sauce (or Pizza Sauce, see page 208) to your cooked rice.

This meal ends with a low-fat dessert: apple sprinkled with a touch of cinnamon and icing sugar. Instead of apple, you could have an orange or ½ cup (125 mL) of cantaloupe, melon or grapes.

If you are having this meal in a restaurant, remember to ask for light salad dressing on the side.

Food Choices	Large Meal	Small Meal
Carbohydrate	4½	2½
Meat and Alternatives	4	2½
Fat	3	2
Nutritional Info	**Large Meal**	**Small Meal**
Carbohydrate	80 g	64 g
Fiber	9 g	8 g

Your Dinner Menu	Large Meal (730 calories)	Small Meal (550 calories)
Shish Kebab	1 made with 4 cubes of beef	1 made with 3 cubes of beef
White or brown rice	⅔ cup (150 mL)	⅔ cup (150 mL)
Greek Salad with dressing	1 serving	1 serving
Crusty white bun	1	–
Margarine	1 tsp (5 mL)	–
Cinnamon apple rings	½ medium apple with ½ tsp (2 mL) icing sugar plus cinnamon	½ medium apple with ½ tsp (2 mL) icing sugar plus cinnamon

SMALL MEAL

Roti with Curried Filling

Rotis and chapatis are flat East Indian breads made from flour and water. Rotis or chapatis can be bought ready-made. If you can't find rotis for this recipe, wrap ¾ cup (175 mL) filling in 2 chapatis or one 10-inch (25 cm) tortilla. Two-thirds of a cup (150 mL) of rice could also replace a roti shell.

In the Caribbean, rotis are served folded around a filling of curried meat, chicken or beans and potatoes.

Plantains
Plantains look like large green bananas (see photograph). But unlike a banana, plantains need to be cooked before eating. Plantain is ready to use when the skin has turned partly black on the outside. Then you can peel it, cut it in strips and boil it until soft. Next, lightly brush it with margarine and roast or broil it in the oven. It can also be boiled, then fried in a nonstick pan. It is served as a starchy vegetable (like corn or potatoes).

Curried Chickpeas and Potato Filling

**Makes 3 cups (750 mL)
(enough for 4 rotis)**

¼ cup (50 mL) water	
1 tsp (5 mL) olive or vegetable oil	
1 medium onion, chopped	
2 cloves garlic, finely chopped or crushed	
1 tbsp (15 mL) curry powder (mild or hot)	
Dash of hot pepper sauce or chili powder	
2 cups (500 mL) diced cooked potatoes	
19-oz (540 mL) can chickpeas, including juice	

Per ¾ cup (175 mL)	
Calories	257
Carbohydrate	50 g
Fiber	8 g
Protein	9 g
Fat, total	3 g
Fat, saturated	0 g
Cholesterol	0 mg
Sodium	415 mg

1. Heat the water and oil in a heavy pot and add the onions, garlic, curry powder and hot pepper sauce. Cook at low heat until the onions are soft.
2. Add the cooked potatoes and canned chickpeas with juice and cook for 30 minutes. Cool and put in the fridge overnight.

Making the Rotis
The next day, reheat the filling and place ¾ cup (175 mL) in the middle of each 3 oz (90 g) roti. Fold one side over the mixture, then the other. Fold ends toward the center to make a neat package. Turn it over on the plate so the folds are underneath. Microwave on high for 3 to 4 minutes, or heat in a hot oven for 30 minutes.

This meal is served with carrot sticks and Cucumbers in Yogurt. The large meal also has plantains.

Cucumbers in Yogurt

Makes 2 servings

1 medium cucumber, peeled and thinly sliced	
¼ cup (50 mL) fat-free plain yogurt	
Mint or paprika to taste	
Dash of vinegar, lemon juice or lime juice	
½ tsp (2 mL) garlic powder or 1 garlic clove, finely chopped	

Per serving	
Calories	24
Carbohydrate	4 g
Fiber	1 g
Protein	2 g
Fat, total	0 g
Fat, saturated	0 g
Cholesterol	1 mg
Sodium	23 mg

1. Combine all ingredients in a bowl.

The dessert for this meal is Coconut Meringues, which are made with sugar, but no fat — so the calories of this dessert are low. Two of these meringues have about the same amount of sugar and calories as a small piece of fruit.

Coconut Meringues

Makes twenty-eight 2-inch (5 cm) meringues

Per cookie	
Calories	32
Carbohydrate	7 g
Fiber	0 g
Protein	1 g
Fat, total	0 g
Fat, saturated	0 g
Cholesterol	0 mg
Sodium	8 mg

1 cup (250 mL) sugar

$\frac{1}{4}$ tsp (1 mL) cream of tartar

4 egg whites, at room temperature

$\frac{1}{2}$ tsp (2 mL) coconut extract

1 tbsp (15 mL) unsweetened coconut (optional)

1. In a small bowl, mix the sugar with the cream of tartar.
2. Beat the egg whites until stiff. Add the sugar and cream of tartar mixture slowly and continue beating until the mixture forms stiff peaks. Beat in the coconut extract.
3. Drop heaping tablespoonfuls (15 mL) onto 2 ungreased cookie sheets. Sprinkle the coconut on top of the meringues, if desired. Bake at 200°F (100°C) for 2 hours. After $1\frac{1}{2}$ hours, check to see if they are ready. They should be dry when you poke them with a skewer or toothpick. When they're ready, turn the oven off and let them sit in the oven for another 2 hours.
4. Once cooled, store in a cookie jar or plastic container.

Food Choices	Large Meal	Small Meal
Carbohydrate	$6\frac{1}{2}$	4
Meat and Alternatives	1	1
Fat	1	–

Nutritional Info	Large Meal	Small Meal
Carbohydrate	133 g	100 g
Fiber	14 g	11 g

Your Dinner Menu	Large Meal (730 calories)	Small Meal (550 calories)
Curried Chickpea & Potato Roti	1 roti	1 roti
Roasted plantain (brushed lightly with 1 tsp/5 mL margarine)	$\frac{1}{3}$ small	–
Carrot sticks	1 medium carrot	$\frac{1}{3}$ medium carrot
Cucumbers in Yogurt	1 serving	1 serving
Coconut Meringues	2	1

SMALL MEAL

DINNER 31

Tandoori Chicken & Rice

I fell in love with tandoori chicken when I lived in Kenya. This delicious meal is spicy but not hot. The chicken is coated in a tasty low-fat coating and then broiled or barbecued.

Tandoori chicken can be served with either:
- *rice, as shown in the photograph (my favorite is basmati rice)*
- *chapati or naan bread (East Indian breads)*

This recipe is also delicious when made with curry powder instead of the tandoori mix. If you use curry powder, the sauce will be a golden curry color. The tandoori mix will make the sauce reddish.

It is important to boil the sauce for 5 minutes. Raw chicken has a lot of bacteria, and boiling will make the sauce safe to eat.

Tandoori Chicken and Sauce

Makes 5 large or 8 small servings

Sauce:

1½ cups (375 mL) plain (white) skim milk yogurt

1½ tbsp (22 mL) store-bought tandoori spice mix

1½ tbsp (22 mL) vinegar

1½ tbsp (22 mL) lemon juice

2½ lbs (1 kg) chicken pieces (weight with bones and skin), skin removed

Per 1 tbsp (15 mL) sauce	
Calories	7
Carbohydrate	1 g
Fiber	0 g
Protein	1 g
Fat, total	0 g
Fat, saturated	0 g
Cholesterol	0 mg
Sodium	9 mg

1. In a large bowl or pot, mix all the ingredients for the sauce.
2. Make some small cuts in each chicken piece so the yogurt sauce can flavor the meat. Add the chicken to the bowl or pot, making sure that it is covered with sauce. Cover and place in the fridge for at least 4 hours or overnight.
3. Gently shake any extra sauce from the chicken and barbecue or place on a rack in a pan and grill in the oven (about 5 inches/12.5 cm from the grill). Cook for 10 to 15 minutes on each side, until well done.
4. Put the leftover sauce in a small, heavy pan and boil for 5 minutes. Give each person a small dish of this sauce for dunking their chicken and putting on their rice.

Poppadums

If you've never had poppadums, you don't know what you're missing! They can be bought in large food stores and in specialty food stores. They are 5 to 7 inches (12.5 to 17.5 cm) round and come in mild or hot (spicy). All you need to do is place them under a hot broiler and in 1 or 2 minutes they will bubble and turn a golden brown. Broil both sides. Or run them quickly under tap water to wet them and then pop them in the microwave on High for about 40 seconds. These crunchy treats are great with a curry meal or can be eaten as a snack.

A nice finish to this meal is a small piece of tropical fruit, such as mango or papaya.

Indian Spiced Tea

Makes 5 cups (1.25 L)

1 tea bag

3 cardamom pods

1 2-inch (5 cm) stick cinnamon

½ tsp (2 mL) lemon juice

2½ cups (625 mL) boiling water

2½ cups (625 mL) hot skim milk

Per 1 cup (250 mL)	
Calories	44
Carbohydrate	6 g
Fiber	0 g
Protein	4 g
Fat, total	0 g
Fat, saturated	0 g
Cholesterol	2 mg
Sodium	67 mg

Serve this meal with chai tea. For an alternative to the commercial chai tea in a bag, try this homemade version.

1. Place tea, cardamom, cinnamon and lemon juice in your teapot. Add the boiling water and let steep for 4 minutes. Remove the bag, the cardamom and the cinnamon from the pot.
2. Serve the tea with an equal part of hot skim milk and, if you want, 1 teaspoon (5 mL) of sugar, honey or low-calorie sweetener.

Food Choices	Large Meal	Small Meal
Carbohydrate	5½	4½
Meat and Alternatives	5	3

Nutritional Info	Large Meal	Small Meal
Carbohydrate	95 g	75 g
Fiber	6 g	6 g

Your Dinner Menu	Large Meal (730 calories)	Small Meal (550 calories)
Tandoori Chicken	1 large leg	1 small leg
Tandoori Sauce	4 tbsp (60 mL)	2 tbsp (25 mL)
Rice (basmati)	1 cup (250 mL)	⅔ cup (150 mL)
Sliced raw vegetables	As desired	As desired
Poppadums	2	2
Mango	½ medium	½ medium
Indian Spiced Tea	1 cup (250 mL)	1 cup (250 mL)

SMALL MEAL

SMALL MEAL

Thai Chicken

Thai Chicken

Makes 3½ cups (875 mL)
(3½ large servings or 4½ small servings)

Per 1 cup (250 mL)	
Calories	311
Carbohydrate	20 g
Fiber	2 g
Protein	32 g
Fat, total	11 g
Fat, saturated	3 g
Cholesterol	88 mg
Sodium	620 mg

6 chicken thighs (or 4 small breasts), skin and visible fat removed and bones cut out, cut into strips

1 small onion, chopped

2 tbsp (25 mL) water

¾ cup (175 mL) salsa (mild or hot)

2 tbsp (25 mL) chopped fresh cilantro

3 tbsp (45 mL) light (reduced-fat) peanut butter

1 tbsp (15 mL) oyster sauce

1 cup (250 mL) skim (non-fat) evaporated canned milk

1 tsp (5 mL) cornstarch

Cilantro and lime wedges, for garnish

1. Place the chicken strips and chopped onions with the water in a large nonstick frying pan. Cook on medium-low heat until there is no pink inside the chicken.
2. In a bowl, mix together the salsa, cilantro, peanut butter and oyster sauce.
3. In another bowl, whisk the cornstarch into the evaporated milk until well blended.
4. Add the salsa mixture to the chicken, then pour in the milk. Stir until the sauce boils and thickens.

Poppy Seed Spinach Salad

Makes 2 servings

Per serving	
Calories	51
Carbohydrate	7 g
Fiber	3 g
Protein	3 g
Fat, total	2 g
Fat, saturated	0 g
Cholesterol	0 mg
Sodium	41 mg

⅓ of a 10-oz (300 g) bag of washed spinach

1 medium tomato, cut into small wedges

¼ small red onion, sliced into rings (optional)

½ cup (125 mL) sliced fresh strawberries

1 tbsp (15 mL) sliced almonds, lightly toasted

Sprinkle of poppy seeds, for topping (optional)

Light creamy poppy seed salad dressing (2 tbsp/25 mL for large meal and 1 tbsp/15 mL for small meal)

1. Wash spinach and arrange in two salad bowls.
2. Place the other ingredients on top of the spinach.

Winter Fruit Cream

Makes 3 servings

14-oz (398 mL) can of fruit, drained

1 tbsp (15 mL) brown sugar

⅛ tsp (0.5 mL) cinnamon

⅓ cup (75 mL) fat-free sour cream

Per serving	
Calories	77
Carbohydrate	19 g
Fiber	1 g
Protein	1 g
Fat, total	0 g
Fat, saturated	0 g
Cholesterol	0 mg
Sodium	45 mg

1. Place the fruit pieces in a small casserole dish or, if you have three small ovenproof dessert bowls, divide the fruit between the bowls.
2. Mix the brown sugar and cinnamon together in a small bowl. Place about half of the sugar and cinnamon mixture on top of the fruit.
3. Add the sour cream on top of the fruit and sugar. Then top the sour cream with the remainder of the sugar and cinnamon.
4. Place under a hot grill and grill for about 4 to 6 minutes, until it's bubbling around the edges and caramelized on top.

Summer Fruit Cream

Makes 3 servings

1½ to 2 cups (375 to 500 mL) sliced or chopped fresh fruit

1 tbsp (15 mL) brown sugar

⅛ tsp (0.5 mL) cinnamon

⅓ cup (75 mL) fat-free sour cream

Per serving	
Calories	75
Carbohydrate	18 g
Fiber	2 g
Protein	1 g
Fat, total	0 g
Fat, saturated	0 g
Cholesterol	0 mg
Sodium	42 mg

1. Divide the fruit between three dessert bowls.
2. Mix brown sugar, cinnamon and sour cream together and place on top of each serving.

__Healthy desserts__
Dessert is not just a sweet end to a meal, it can contribute to your day's nutrition. Here are two nutritious fruit desserts. Winter Fruit Cream is made with canned fruit (such as apricots, peaches or pears), and is heated under the grill. Summer Fruit Cream is made with fresh fruit (such as sliced strawberries or kiwis, blueberries, orange pieces, melon slices, pomegranate seeds or thin apple slices) and served cold. Both are equally sensational.

Food Choices	Large Meal	Small Meal
Carbohydrate	5	3½
Meat and Alternatives	3½	3
Fat	1	½

Nutritional Info	Large Meal	Small Meal
Carbohydrate	96 g	74 g
Fiber	8 g	7 g

Your Dinner Menu	Large Meal (730 calories)	Small Meal (550 calories)
Thai Chicken	1 cup (250 mL)	¾ cup (175 mL)
Noodles or rice, cooked	1 cup (250 mL)	⅔ cup (150 mL)
Poppy Seed Spinach Salad	1 serving	1 serving
Light creamy poppy seed salad dressing	2 tbsp (25 mL)	1 tbsp (15 mL)
Winter Fruit Cream or Summer Fruit Cream	1 serving	1 serving

SMALL MEAL

SMALL MEAL

DINNER 35

Sub Sandwich

Sub sandwiches can be a healthy fast-food dinner. What is not healthy are the portion sizes, the extra sandwich sauces, the large-sized soft drinks, juices or sweetened milk, the potato chips and super-sized cookies or brownies.

Sugar in Beverages

When eating out, your choice of beverage can add many extra calories (from sugar and fat) to your meal. I suggest water or a diet drink with this meal. The table below shows a breakdown of the amount of sugar in beverages.

Teaspoons of sugar in a 16-ounce (2 cups/500 mL) serving of a beverage

No Sugar	• Tap water, plain bottled water, mineral water or soda water • Diet soft drinks, Sugar Free Kool-Aid, Sugar Free Tang or Crystal Light • Tea, herbal tea, perked or instant coffee, no sugar added
3–6 teaspoons (15–30 mL)	• Sweetened (flavored) instant coffee powders (3); caffe latte (4) • Tomato juice or V8 (5) • White milk (5)
7–10 teaspoons (35–50 mL)	• Mountain Dew (7), Sprite (8), ginger ale (10) or tonic water (10) • Kool-Aid made with sugar (8) • Powerade sports drink (9) • Instant Breakfast, made with milk, no sugar added (10) • Iced tea, made from instant powder with sugar (10) • Grapefruit juice, unsweetened (10)
11–15 teaspoons (55–75 mL)	• Orange juice (11–13) or apple juice (14), both unsweetened • Tang (11), colas (12), cream soda (15) or fruit drinks (15) • Chocolate milk (12) • Slushes or Slurpees (13) • Rice beverage (12) or soy milk (4–13), both sweetened • Iced specialty coffees (13) • Many energy drinks (11–15)
16–20 teaspoons (80–100 mL)	• Pineapple juice (16) or grape juice (18), both unsweetened • Cranberry juice cocktail (17) • Eggnog, non-alcoholic (16) • Commercial shakes (16) or fruit smoothies (18+) • Instant Breakfast, regular, made with sugar (16) • Boost (19)
21–34 teaspoons (105–170 mL)	• Frappuccino malt coffee (21) • Prune juice, unsweetened (21) • Triple Thick Shake (22) or Fruit Smoothie Supreme (26) • Gatorade energy drink (24)

Nutrient Guides

Visit the website of the fast-food restaurant where you like to eat most often. There you will find the nutrient guides for their meals. You can also ask for the information at the counter. Keep in mind that they may not list the extras, such as mayonnaise, that we add to our sub sandwiches. Also, products like potato chips or corn chips come in various package sizes. A 1½-oz (45 g) bag of regular chips will be around 230 calories. Baked chips contain about 1 teaspoon (5 mL) less fat per 1½-oz (45 g) bag.

If you want to make a quick sub sandwich at home that would equal the same calories as a commercial 6-inch sub, here are the portions.

Homemade 6-inch (15 cm) Sub Sandwich

(made with 3 oz/90 g roast chicken)

6-inch (15 cm) long whole wheat sub bun

3 oz (90 g) thinly sliced meat of your choice

1½ oz (45 g) sliced light cheese of your choice

A variety of vegetables of your choice

Black pepper

1 tbsp (15 mL) light mayonnaise or 2 tbsp (25 mL) fat-free mayonnaise

1 tbsp (15 mL) fat-free honey mustard

Per sandwich

Calories 484
Carbohydrate . . . . . 40 g
Fiber. . . . . .6 g
Protein . . . . 44 g
Fat, total. . . . . 16 g
Fat, saturated . . . . . . 8 g
Cholesterol . . . . 105 mg
Sodium . . . . . . .773 mg

1. Cut the sub bun in half crosswise. If desired, toast under the broiler.
2. Evenly spread the meat and cheese on the bottom half of the bun.
3. Add the vegetables, pepper and condiments. Cover with the top half of the bun.

To reduce your intake of sodium and fat, eat half the bag of chips — or share it with a friend!

Cold cuts contain a lot of salt. For example, 1 oz (30 g) of ham has about 300 mg of sodium. In comparison, 1 oz (30 g) of leftover roast chicken has only 25 mg of sodium, so use leftover roast meat when you can.

Food Choices	Large Meal	Small Meal
Carbohydrate	4½	3
Meat and Alternatives	4½	4½
Fat	3	1
Nutritional Info	**Large Meal**	**Small Meal**
Carbohydrate	77 g	49 g
Fiber	10 g	7 g

Your Dinner Menu	Large Meal (730 calories)	Small Meal (550 calories)
Homemade Sub Sandwich or Purchased sub sandwich	1 sandwich (6 inch/15 cm) or up to 450 calories, plus 1 tbsp (15 mL) each light mayonnaise and honey mustard	1 sandwich (6 inch/15 cm) or up to 450 calories, plus 1 tbsp (15 mL) each light mayonnaise and honey mustard
1 bag of chips or nachos or 1 large cookie	1 choice (200–210 calories)	–
Diet drink	Medium	Medium

249

SMALL MEAL

Beef Parmesan

My son created this zippy, nutritious meal that can be cooked in a toaster oven, regular oven or frying pan. This meal has lots of variations because you can use the Classic Beef Patties below, or frozen beef patties, breaded chicken cutlets, veal cutlets, pork cutlets or pounded minute steak. Once cooked, simply top the meat or chicken piece with pasta sauce and shredded cheese.

This meal is served with Low-Fat Mashed Potatoes (see Dinner 8), broccoli, a tossed salad and ice cream for dessert.

Pasta sauces vary in calories

Some pasta sauces have more oil or sugar added. Check the Nutrition Facts on the pasta sauce label and look for a mid-range to lower-calorie choice, such as 30 to 60 calories per $1/2$-cup (125 mL) serving.

Seasoning salt

If you add $1/2$ tsp (2 mL) Hy's Seasoning Salt to the recipe, you will add 85 mg more sodium per patty.

Beef Parmesan

For each patty:

	Per patty with toppings
Meat patty or cutlet of your choice	Calories 278
3 tbsp (45 mL) pasta sauce	Carbohydrate . . . . . 10 g Fiber . . . . 0 g Protein . . . . 24 g
Dash of hot pepper sauce or hot pepper flakes	Fat, total . . . . 15 g Fat, saturated . . . . . . 6 g Cholesterol . . . . . 95 mg
$1\frac{1}{2}$ tbsp (22 mL) grated parmesan, cheddar or mozzarella cheese	Sodium . . . . 507 mg

1. If using a store-bought frozen patty or cutlet, cook in a frying pan, oven or barbecue according to the package directions. If making homemade beef patties, cook according to directions below.
2. Heat pasta sauce in the microwave or on the stovetop over medium heat until hot and bubbling. Add hot pepper sauce or flakes, if using.
3. Place meat patty or cutlet on your plate and top with the pasta sauce, then the shredded cheese.

Classic Beef Patties

Makes 10 large patties

	Per patty
12 unsalted soda crackers, crumbled	Calories . . . . 182 Carbohydrate . . . . . . 4 g
2 lbs (1 kg) lean ground beef	Fiber . . . . 0 g Protein . . . . 18 g
2 eggs	Fat, total . . . . 10 g
1 small onion, finely chopped	Fat, saturated . . . . . . 4 g Cholesterol . . . . . 85 mg
2 tsp (10 mL) Worcestershire sauce	Sodium . . . . 94 mg
Hy's Seasoning Salt (optional)	
$\frac{1}{4}$ tsp (1 mL) pepper	

1. Add all ingredients to a large mixing bowl. Mix together with your hands.
2. Form into 10 patties and place on a plate or tray.
3. Fry patties in a pan over medium heat, or cook under a grill or on the barbecue, until no longer pink inside.

Different Kinds of Ice Cream

Limit or Avoid Rich Ice Cream

Decadent ice creams get their reputation for a reason. Up to a third of their calories comes from unhealthy saturated fat, and a $\frac{1}{2}$-cup (125 mL) serving can have up to 4 teaspoons (20 mL) of sugar. At 200 to 300 (or more) calories per $\frac{1}{2}$ cup (125 mL), they contain up to double the calories of regular ice cream.

Other Ice Creams

Low-fat or sugar-free ice creams (at 100 to 120 calories per $\frac{1}{2}$ cup/125 mL) are a little lower than regular ice cream at 125 to 150 calories for the same amount. Frozen yogurt with no more than 3 grams of fat per $\frac{1}{2}$ cup (125 mL) contains around 100 to 110 calories in that amount.

Bowl Sizes Affect How Much You Eat

When you eat from a smaller bowl, you will eat less. Take a look at these three bowls, which each hold a $\frac{1}{2}$-cup (125 mL) scoop of regular ice cream. By putting the ice cream in the small bowl at the bottom, it looks more filling. If you use the large bowl at the top, you just might fill it up with three or four scoops of ice cream, and you would overeat.

Food Choices	Large Meal	Small Meal
Carbohydrate	3	2
Meat and Alternatives	5	$3\frac{1}{2}$
Nutritional Info	Large Meal	Small Meal
Carbohydrate	85 g	61 g
Fiber	6 g	4 g

Your Dinner Menu	Large Meal (730 calories)	Small Meal (550 calories)
Beef Parmesan	$1\frac{1}{2}$ patties with sauce and cheese	1 patty with sauce and cheese
Low-Fat Mashed Potatoes	1 cup (250 mL)	$\frac{1}{2}$ cup (125 mL)
Broccoli	1 to 2 cups (250 to 500 mL)	1 to 2 cups (250 to 500 mL)
Tossed salad	Medium	Medium
Fat-free Italian salad dressing	1 tbsp (15 mL)	1 tbsp (15 mL)
Frozen yogurt or ice cream (light or regular)	$\frac{1}{2}$ cup (125 mL)	$\frac{1}{2}$ cup (125 mL)

SMALL MEAL

Santa Fe Salad

This flavorful and colorful salad includes corn, beans and chicken, and is inspired by Mexican-American cuisine. It is served with tortilla chips and Banana Bread.

Santa Fe Salad

Makes 4 servings

Per serving
Calories 348
Carbohydrate . . . . . 43 g
Fiber. . . . . 9 g
Protein . . . . 29 g
Fat, total . . . . 8 g
Fat, saturated . . . . . . 4 g
Cholesterol . . . . . 60 mg
Sodium . . . . 860 mg

12-oz (341 mL) can of corn

19-ounce (540 mL) can of black beans, rinsed in cold water and drained well

1 tbsp (15 mL) finely chopped fresh cilantro or parsley

2 to 3 green onions, chopped

1 red pepper, cut into thin 1-inch (2.5 cm) slices

½ head of lettuce, torn into bite-size pieces

½ cup (125 mL) shredded or grated cheese

3 tbsp (45 mL) light coleslaw dressing

10 oz (300 g) chicken breasts or thighs, boneless and skin removed, sliced into thin pieces

2 tbsp (25 mL) hickory smoke barbecue sauce

1. In a large bowl, gently toss corn, black beans, cilantro, green onions, red pepper, lettuce and cheese. Mix in the coleslaw dressing. Divide salad onto four dinner plates (or large salad bowls).
2. Over medium heat, cook the chicken pieces in a nonstick pan with about 2 tablespoons (25 mL) of water. When the chicken is no longer pink inside, add the barbecue sauce. Reduce the heat and simmer for a couple of minutes.
3. Divide the chicken between the four plates, placing on top of the salad.

Banana Bread is a heart-warming accompaniment to the Santa Fe Salad. It serves as a starch and a sweet dessert. An alternative to the Banana Bread is the Irish Currant Cake (Breakfast 15). You can also enjoy the Bran Muffin (Breakfast 7) in place of the Banana Bread. The large meal allows 2 muffins, while the small meal allows 1.

One slice of Banana Bread can be eaten as a large snack (200 calories); see the snack section, pages 276–285. Banana Bread can also nicely substitute for 1 cup (250 mL) of Rice Pudding (Dinner 5).

For a lower-carbohydrate alternative to this meal, add a few extra pieces of chicken to your salad and skip the banana bread.

Banana Bread

Makes 12 slices

2¼ cups (550 mL) flour

1 tbsp (15 mL) baking powder

½ tsp (2 mL) salt

½ tsp (2 mL) nutmeg

2 tbsp (25 mL) margarine or butter

½ cup (125 mL) sugar

1 large egg

¼ cup (50 mL) skim milk

3 small bananas

½ cup (125 mL) raisins

¼ cup (50 mL) chopped walnuts or pecans

Per slice

Calories	204
Carbohydrate	39 g
Fiber	2 g
Protein	4 g
Fat, total	4 g
Fat, saturated	1 g
Cholesterol	16 mg
Sodium	197 mg

1. Mix flour with baking powder, salt and nutmeg in a medium bowl.
2. In a large bowl, cream margarine and sugar with a wooden spoon. Beat in the egg and milk until smooth.
3. In a small bowl, mash the bananas with a fork.
4. Add mashed bananas and the flour mixture to the large bowl, and stir together. Then add the nuts and raisins.
5. Scrape into a lightly greased 9- by 5-inch (2 L) loaf pan and bake for 1 hour at 350°F (180°C), until a knife inserted in the center comes out clean. Let cool in the pan, then remove and cut into 12 slices.

Food Choices	Large Meal	Small Meal
Carbohydrate	5	4½
Meat and Alternatives	3½	3½
Fat	1½	–

Nutritional Info	Large Meal	Small Meal
Carbohydrate	93 g	88 g
Fiber	12 g	12 g

Your Dinner Menu	Large Meal (730 calories)	Small Meal (550 calories)
Santa Fe Salad	1 serving	1 serving
Tortilla chips	8 chips	5 chips
Banana Bread	1 slice	1 slice
Margarine or butter	1½ tsp (7 mL)	–

SMALL MEAL

DINNER 38

Pork Chop Casserole

This scrumptious and uncomplicated, no-fail casserole will take an hour to cook. After it has cooked for 40 minutes, put the rice on to cook. At this time, prepare the Grilled Tomato halves. They can go into the oven alongside the casserole dish and cook for the last 15 minutes. The plan is to have the rice, pork chops and tomatoes ready at the same time.

Add your favorite soup

This casserole is made with your favorite cream soup, such as cream of mushroom, cream of celery, cream of broccoli or cream of chicken. Choose a low-fat cream soup to help cut back on total fat in your meal.

Pork Chop Casserole

Makes 3 large or 5 small meals

5 pork chops (thin loin cut), total raw weight with bone about 1¾ lbs (875 g)	
1 small onion, thinly sliced	
3 stalks celery, sliced	
10-ounce (284 mL) can low-fat cream soup	

Per pork chop with sauce

Calories	192
Carbohydrate	6 g
Fiber	1 g
Protein	21 g
Fat, total	8 g
Fat, saturated	3 g
Cholesterol	62 mg
Sodium	439 mg

1. Trim the visible fat from the pork chops. Place in a casserole dish. Evenly add the onion and celery on top of the pork chops. Spread the cream soup on top.
2. Bake in a covered casserole dish at 350°F (180°C) for 1 hour, or more if needed, until the pork chops are fork-tender.

Grilled Tomato

Makes 2 servings

1 medium tomato, washed	
1 tsp (5 mL) dry bread crumbs	
1 tsp (5 mL) ground flaxseeds	
2 tsp (10 mL) store-bought pre-grated parmesan cheese	
½ tsp (2 mL) dried oregano	
1 tsp (5 mL) butter or margarine	

Per serving

Calories	51
Carbohydrate	4 g
Fiber	1 g
Protein	2 g
Fat, total	3 g
Fat, saturated	2 g
Cholesterol	7 mg
Sodium	72 mg

1. Cut the tomato in half crosswise. Place cut side up in a casserole or small baking pan.
2. In a small bowl, combine bread crumbs, flaxseeds, parmesan cheese, oregano and butter. Spoon over the open tomato halves and, with the back of the spoon, press down gently.
3. Bake at 350°F (180°C) for 15 minutes. Then put under the broiler until the topping is golden brown. The broiling will only take a minute or less — watch it carefully so it doesn't burn.

Sugar Snap Peas

This meal is served with raw sugar snap peas on the side. These crunchy peas are great raw or lightly steamed. They are low-calorie, with just 14 calories in 10 snap peas. Sugar snap peas can be added anytime to a stir-fry, or sliced and added to a salad or casserole. They are also great as a snack in the middle of the day or in the evening. If you can't find sugar snap peas, you can substitute any other low-calorie vegetable (see page 149).

Mandarins and Cottage Cheese is a simple, delicious dessert.

Mandarins and Cottage Cheese

Makes 4 servings

1 cup (250 mL) canned mandarin orange segments in light syrup, drained	
¾ cup (175 mL) 1% cottage cheese	
Pinch of ground nutmeg	

Per serving

Calories	59
Carbohydrate	9 g
Fiber	0 g
Protein	6 g
Fat, total	0 g
Fat, saturated	0 g
Cholesterol	2 mg
Sodium	180 mg

1. Gently combine the orange pieces and cottage cheese, reserving a few mandarin segments to decorate the top of each serving.
2. Divide among three dessert-size dishes and decorate with the reserved orange segments and nutmeg, if desired.

This meal is served with a cup of antioxidant-rich green tea. Enjoy it without milk and add a small amount of sweetener if you wish.

> **Benefits of tea**
> Black tea and green tea contain heart-healthy antioxidants. Green teas appear to have the greatest health benefit, which will come from drinking tea every day. There are significantly fewer antioxidants in tea when it is decaffeinated, since the process of removing the caffeine also removes many of the antioxidants. However, if you wish to limit or avoid caffeine, feel free to choose a cup of decaffeinated black tea or coffee, or one of the many delicious flavors of herbal tea.

Food Choices	Large Meal	Small Meal
Carbohydrate	5	3½
Meat and Alternatives	5	3½

Nutritional Info	Large Meal	Small Meal
Carbohydrate	86 g	68 g
Fiber	5 g	4 g

Your Dinner Menu	Large Meal (730 calories)	Small Meal (550 calories)
Pork chops with sauce	1½ chops	1 chop
Rice	1⅓ cups (325 mL)	1 cup (250 mL)
Grilled Tomato	1 half	1 half
Sugar snap peas	15	15
Mandarins and Cottage Cheese	1 serving	1 serving
Green tea	1 cup (250 mL)	1 cup (250 mL)

SMALL MEAL

DINNER 39

Shrimp Linguini

Linguini is a flat pasta noodle that, in southern Italy, is traditionally served with a clam or seafood sauce. I have chosen shrimp for the sauce, as it is a delight to eat and is readily available, precooked and frozen. The Shrimp Linguini Sauce will take about 30 minutes to prepare and cook. The Shrimp Linguini is served with Caesar Salad, and the beverage is a refreshing Italian Iced Cream Soda.

Cooking pasta

Remember to cook your pasta according to the directions on the package so that it will be ready at the same time as the sauce. However, when you cook it, it's not necessary to add salt.

Shrimp Linguini Sauce

Makes 4 cups (1 L)

2 tsp (10 mL) olive or vegetable oil

⅓ cup (75 mL) water

1 small onion, chopped

3 large cloves garlic, minced

1 cup (250 mL) sliced fresh mushrooms (or one 10-oz/284 mL can, drained)

2 tbsp (25 mL) flour

1 packet (4.5 g) reduced-sodium chicken bouillon powder

⅛ tsp (0.5 mL) ground pepper

1 tsp (5 mL) dried dill

1¾ cups (425 mL) skim milk

½ red or green pepper, cut into 1-inch (2.5 cm) thick strips, or ½ cup (125 mL) other vegetables of your choice

10 oz (300 g) cooked frozen shrimp, thawed, shells and tails removed

¾ cup (175 mL) shredded Italian four-cheese blend, or cheese of your choice

Per 1 cup (250 mL)	
Calories	241
Carbohydrate	14 g
Fiber	1 g
Protein	27 g
Fat, total	9 g
Fat, saturated	4 g
Cholesterol	133 mg
Sodium	482 mg

1. Add olive oil, water, onion and garlic to a large pan, and cook over medium heat until soft.
2. Meanwhile, in a small pan, sauté the mushrooms in a bit of water over medium heat until soft. Drain off the water and set the mushrooms aside.
3. In a small bowl, mix the flour, bouillon powder, ground pepper and dill. Add this mixture to the onion mixture and stir until the flour is absorbed.
4. Gradually whisk in the milk and cook, stirring constantly, until the mixture thickens slightly, about 5 minutes. Do not let boil. Mix in vegetables and shrimp, and cook, stirring often, until vegetables are tender, about 5 minutes.
5. Stir in the mushrooms and shredded cheese until melted. The sauce will thicken up now.
6. Serve over cooked linguini.

Caesar salad is usually made with dark green romaine lettuce. Dark salad greens are rich in folic acid, a nutrient that is essential for pregnant mothers, but also important for everybody's heart health.

Caesar Salad

For 1 serving:

2 cups (500 mL) dark salad greens, torn into bite-size pieces

2 tbsp (25 mL) shredded fresh parmesan cheese or 1 tbsp (15 mL) grated dried parmesan

¼ cup (50 mL) croutons

Squirt of fresh lemon juice (optional)

Fat-free Caesar salad dressing

Per serving	
Calories	88
Carbohydrate	9 g
Fiber	2 g
Protein	6 g
Fat, total	3 g
Fat, saturated	2 g
Cholesterol	7 mg
Sodium	231 mg

1. Combine greens, cheese, croutons and lemon juice, if using.
2. Top with Caesar salad dressing (see menu box for amount).

You'll save money making this salad from scratch at home, and it's really easy when you use ready-made croutons and a low-fat salad dressing. I don't recommend the all-in-one Caesar salad kits, because the dressing is usually high in calories. However, if the kit is labeled as having a low-fat salad dressing, it would be a good choice.

This cool and delightful beverage is best with crushed ice; however, it can be served over ice cubes. Orange Crush can be substituted for cream soda, if you prefer. This beverage counts as a light dessert for this meal because of the sugar in the regular soft drink. Diet sodas are not recommended in this recipe, because they will cause the milk to curdle.

Italian Iced Cream Soda

Makes one 12-oz (375 mL) serving

½ cup (125 mL) crushed ice

¾ cup (175 mL) cream soda (6 oz)

¼ cup (50 mL) skim milk

Per serving	
Calories	116
Carbohydrate	28 g
Fiber	0 g
Protein	2 g
Fat, total	0 g
Fat, saturated	0 g
Cholesterol	1 mg
Sodium	57 mg

1. Pour ice into a tall glass.
2. Slowly pour the cream soda over the ice, then add the milk. Stir and enjoy.

Food Choices	Large Meal	Small Meal
Carbohydrate	6½	5
Meat and Alternatives	3	2½
Nutritional Info	**Large Meal**	**Small Meal**
Carbohydrate	112 g	89 g
Fiber	7 g	5 g

Your Dinner Menu	Large Meal (730 calories)	Small Meal (550 calories)
Shrimp Linguini Sauce	1 cup (250 mL)	¾ cup (175 mL)
Cooked pasta (linguini)	1½ cups (375 mL)	1 cup (250 mL)
Caesar Salad	1 serving	1 serving
Caesar salad dressing, fat-free	1 tbsp (15 mL)	1 tbsp (15 mL)
Italian Iced Cream Soda	12 oz (375 mL)	12 oz (375 mL)

SMALL MEAL

DINNER 40

Chicken Cordon Bleu

Cordon Bleu is French for "Blue Ribbon," which is a famous cooking school in France. Chicken Cordon Bleu has been adapted from the classic French Veal Cordon Bleu.

This dinner includes sweet potatoes, Sesame Vegetables and a small salad. For dessert, treat yourself to the exquisite Cream Cheese Pomegranate Burst (recipe on page 270).

recipe on page 270

Chicken Cordon Bleu

Makes 3 large or 4 small pieces

Per small piece	
Calories	278
Carbohydrate	6 g
Fiber	0 g
Protein	39 g
Fat, total	10 g
Fat, saturated	5 g
Cholesterol	150 mg
Sodium	398 mg

¼ cup (50 mL) fine dry bread crumbs or flour

Shake of salt and pepper

1 egg

2 slices of ham (½ oz/15 g for each chicken breast)

3 slices of part-skim mozzarella cheese (¾ oz/23 g for each chicken breast)

3 large or 4 small boneless skinless chicken breasts (14 oz/420 g total)

1 tbsp (15 mL) butter or margarine

1. Mix bread crumbs with the salt and pepper in a bowl.
2. In another bowl, beat the egg with a fork.
3. Slice the ham and cheese into four portions and lay on a plate.
4. Cut each chicken breast in half crosswise, but not all the way through.
5. Inside each piece of chicken, tuck a slice of ham and cheese. Pull the top flap of chicken over to cover the ham and cheese. Dip each piece of chicken in the egg, turning to fully coat both sides and the edges in egg. Next, roll the chicken breasts in the bread crumbs. Put the chicken on a dinner plate.
6. Heat the butter in a nonstick pan. Add the chicken pieces to the pan and cover the pan to seal in the heat, as the chicken is quite thick and needs to cook all the way through. Cook over medium heat for 5 to 8 minutes, until nicely browned on one side. Then reduce the heat and cook the other side for 4 to 6 minutes, or until there is no pink inside the chicken.

Sweet Potatoes

See Dinner 10 for information about sweet potatoes. For mashed sweet potatoes, poke the potato with a fork and microwave for about 5 minutes, or peel the potato, cut into 2-inch (5 cm) pieces and boil until tender, about 15 minutes. Cooking time will vary depending on the size of the potato. Mash with a small amount of milk, if desired.

Sesame Vegetables provides an easy way to add flavor and texture to steamed vegetables. Make this recipe with your favorite vegetables; I've used parsnips and yellow and green zucchini. For convenience, you can use frozen mixed vegetables.

Sesame Vegetables

Makes 4 servings

1 tbsp (15 mL) sesame seeds

2 to 3 cups (500 to 750 mL) sliced or diced vegetables

1 tsp (5 mL) olive oil, margarine or butter

1 tsp (5 mL) brown sugar

Per serving	
Calories	56
Carbohydrate	8 g
Fiber	2 g
Protein	2 g
Fat, total	2 g
Fat, saturated	0 g
Cholesterol	0 mg
Sodium	4 mg

Instead of sesame seeds, an equal amount of sunflower seeds and a squirt of lemon juice is delicious on vegetables.

1. Toast sesame seeds in the microwave for 2 to 3 minutes, stirring several times. Or put the sesame seeds in a dry frying pan and toast for a few minutes over medium heat, stirring constantly, until lightly browned.
2. Steam or boil the vegetables until tender-crisp. Drain water.
3. Add the olive oil and brown sugar to the vegetables and mix gently. Then add the toasted sesame seeds to coat the vegetables.

Meal continued on next page.

SMALL MEAL

Snacks

Snacks

In this section you will find photographs of four groups of snacks. The groups are low-calorie snacks, small snacks, medium snacks and large snacks. The calories for each snack within each group are about the same. The number of snacks you choose will depend on how many calories a day you want. Look at the chart on page 8 that shows the calories of the small and large meals and of different snacks.

For most of us it's good to choose no more than three of the small, medium or large snacks a day.

Three small snacks add up to 150 calories, three medium snacks add up to 300 calories and three large snacks add up to 600 calories.

Low-calorie snacks:

- These snacks have just 20 calories or less. These foods are not fattening. A few of these a day will have little effect on your weight. You may add them to your meals or snacks.

Small snacks:

- These snacks have 50 calories.

Medium snacks:

- These snacks have 100 calories.
- Two small snacks would equal one medium snack.

Large snacks:

- These snacks have 200 calories.
- Two medium snacks, or four small snacks, would equal one large snack.

Remember to drink water when you have a snack. And try to avoid late-night snacking.

Remember:
- *1 medium snack = 2 small snacks*

- *1 large snack = 2 medium snacks, or 4 small snacks*

Choose a variety of snacks and you won't get bored. When you eat a snack between meals you will not feel so hungry at meal times. Most of the snacks are low in fat and sugar, just like the meals. A snack made from a milk food will give you important calcium, a vegetable will give you fiber, and a fruit is full of vitamins.

What about eating candy, chocolates and chips and other foods that are made with lots of fat or sugar? It is okay to have a small amount of these once in a while. But these shouldn't be eaten often, as they give you calories but little nutrition. On the photographs on pages 280–285 you will find these kinds of foods marked as occasional snacks. Alcoholic drinks are also marked as an occasional snack choice. Remember the cautions about alcohol (see page 25).

In the photograph of each snack group are snacks with about the same number of calories. However, the snacks have different amounts of sugar or starch, protein or fat.

The grams of total carbohydrates in each snack are listed in red.

In the small, medium and large photographs, you will find:

- starchy snacks, which have mostly starch
- fruit and vegetable snacks, which have natural sugar
- milk snacks have natural milk sugar and protein; and some may have some fat
- mixed snacks, which are a mix of foods from different food groups, such as a starch and a protein
- occasional snacks that are high in fat or sugar, or that have alcohol.

Low-calorie snacks

20 calories or less in each snack

Total carbohydrate in grams is marked in red.

Drinks

1. Water is your best low-calorie snack **0**
2. Diet soft drinks and packaged diet drink mixes **0**
3. Herbal tea **1**
4. Coffee or tea **1** (regular or decaffeinated) — have your coffee or tea black or add a small amount of low-fat milk, skim milk powder or light whitener. Cut back on sugar and try a low-calorie sweetener instead.
5. Bouillon or broth **4** — look for low-salt brands

Additions to your meals or snacks

6. Low-calorie sweeteners **1**
7. Flavorings, such as cocoa, spices and herbs **1**
8. 1 tsp (5 mL) mustard **0**, relish **2** or ketchup **1**
9. Hot pepper sauce **0**
10. Vinegar **1**
11. 1 tbsp (15 mL) salsa **1**
12. 1 tsp (5 mL) honey **7**, jam, jelly or syrup (diet jam or diet syrup will have less sugar) **5**
13. 1 tbsp (15 mL) bran or 1 tbsp flaxseed (2 kinds shown) or 1–2 tsp (5–10 mL) ground flaxseed **2**
14. 1 tbsp (15 mL) whipped or frozen topping (or 1 tbsp/15 mL of light sour cream or 2 tbsp/25 mL of fat-free sour cream) **1–2**
15. 1 tbsp (15 mL) oil-free salad dressing **1–5**

Other Snacks

16. ¼ cup (60 mL) sauerkraut **3**

17. 1 cup (250 mL) salad greens **1**

18. 1 soda cracker **2**

19. ½ cup (125 mL) Jellied Vegetable Salad **2** (see recipe, page 157)

20. ½ tomato **3**

21. ½ cup (125 mL) light gelatin **2**

22. 1 piece sugar-free gum **1** or regular gum **3**

23. 1 mint or small hard candy **4**

24. Several mini-mints **2–3**

25. 1 sugar-free Popsicle **5**

26. 2 green olives **0**

27. 3 radishes **1**

28. 1 dill pickle or 14 pickled hot pepper rings **2**

29. Lemon and lime **4**

30. 1 stalk celery **1**

31. ½ cucumber **3**

279

Small snacks

50 calories in each snack
Total carbohydrate in grams is marked in red.

Vegetables

Always have raw, washed vegetables in the fridge. The vegetables should be ready to eat and easy to grab.

1. ³⁄₄ cup (175 mL) Coleslaw (page 86) **9**
2. 1 stalk celery with 1 tbsp (15 mL) cheese spread **2**
3. Large salad with 1 tbsp (15 mL) fat-free salad dressing **5**
4. 1 medium carrot **8**
5. 1 cup (250 mL) canned tomatoes **10**

Fruit

6. 1 cup (250 mL) strawberries **12**
7. 1 small orange **14**
8. ½ large grapefruit **12**
9. ½ medium apple **11**
10. 1 medium plum **10**
11. 1 medium kiwi **12**
12. 2 prunes (or figs) **11**
13. 2 tbsp (25 mL) raisins **16**
14. 2-inch (5 cm) piece of banana **13**
15. ³⁄₄ cup (175 mL) Light Gelatin with Fruit (page 201) **13**
16. ³⁄₄ cup (175 mL) Stewed Rhubarb (page 125) **10**

Juice

17. 1 cup (250 mL) tomato or vegetable juice **10**
18. ½ cup (125 mL) unsweetened fruit juice **13** (try mixing the juice with some sparkling water or diet ginger ale)

280

Milk snacks

19. ½ cup (125 mL) low-fat fruit yogurt, sweetened with a low-calorie sweetener **8**

20. 1 cup (250 mL) light hot cocoa **8**

21. ½ cup (125 mL) low-fat milk (skim or 1%) **6**

22. 1 light fudge ice cream bar, Revello or Creamsicle (made with a low-calorie sweetener) **12**

Starchy snacks

23. 1 cup (250 mL) puffed wheat cereal **10**

24. 1 cup (250 mL) packaged soup **8**

25. 2 bread sticks **8**

26. 1 rice cake **12**

27. 1 digestive or other plain cookie **8**

28. 2 medium crackers **5**

29. 2 melba toasts **8**

30. 4 soda crackers **9**

31. 1 fiber crispbread **7**

32. 2 Graham wafer halves **11**

33. 2 poppadums **9**

Occasional snacks

34. 1 chocolate chip cookie **7**

35. 1 fig bar **11**

36. ¼ cup (60 mL) (21) fish crackers **7**

37. 3 hard candy mints **12**

38. 5 lifesavers **15**

39. 1 small chocolate **6**

40. 2 marshmallows **12**

41. 3 oz (90 g) dry table wine **3**

Medium snacks

100 calories in each snack
(two small snacks = one medium snack)
Total carbohydrate in grams is marked in red.

Vegetables

1. 2–3 cups (500–750 mL) raw vegetables with 2 tbsp Vegetable Dip (page 189) **20**

Fruit

2. ½ medium cantaloupe **22**
3. 1 cup (250 mL) applesauce **28**
4. 4 pineapple rings plus 2 tbsp (25 mL) juice **24**
5. 1 small banana **27**
6. 3 figs **29**
7. 5 dried apricots **22**
8. 1 pear **25**
9. 1 cup (250 mL) fresh fruit salad **27**
10. 4 thin slices watermelon **22**
11. 1½ cups (375 mL) grapes **24**

Starchy snacks

12. 1 slice raisin bread with 1 tsp (5 mL) of margarine **14**
13. 3 arrowroots or other plain cookies **17**
14. 6 pretzels **24**
15. 1 waffle or crumpet with 1 tsp (5 mL) jam **21**
16. 3 cups (750 mL) air-popped popcorn **19**
17. 1 whole wheat roll with cucumber, tomato, lettuce **19**
18. ⅓ of a 3-oz/80 g package of oriental noodles **20**
19. 1 slice matzo bread **27**
20. 8 baked tortilla chips or other baked chips with 1 tbsp (15 mL) salsa sauce **12**

Mixed snacks

21. ½ pizza bun **13**
22. 1 piece toast with 1 tsp (5 mL) peanut butter **15**
23. ½ cup (125 mL) 1% cottage cheese and ½ tomato **6**
24. 1 cup (250 mL) canned tomatoes and 2 tbsp (25 mL) shredded cheese **10**
25. ⅔ cup (150 mL) round oat cereal and ½ cup (125 mL) low-fat milk **17**

26. ¹⁄₂ cup (125 mL) low-fat milk and 2 gingersnaps **18**
27. 8 jumbo shrimp and 2 tbsp (25 mL) shrimp cocktail sauce **3**
28. 4 soda crackers and ¹⁄₂ oz (15 g) Edam cheese **9**
29. 2 wheat crackers with 1 tbsp (15 mL) light cream cheese **10**

Milk snacks

30. 1 cup (250 mL) low-fat milk (including buttermilk) **12**
31. ³⁄₄ cup (175 mL) light pudding (also nice frozen on a Popsicle stick) **17**
32. ³⁄₄ cup (175 mL) low-fat yogurt **12**

Occasional snacks

33. 1 serving Chocolate Mousse (page 137) and ¹⁄₂ ice wafer **14**
34. 3- by 2-inch (7.5- by 5 cm) piece of rice crispie marshmallow square **21**
35. Low-fat granola bar **21**
36. 1 light beer (12 oz/355 mL) **5**
37. 1¹⁄₂ oz (45 mL) rye, gin, rum, whiskey or other alcohol (mixed with diet pop or water) **0**
38. 1 piece angel food cake **24**
39. 2¹⁄₂ licorice sticks **25**
40. 10 jelly beans **26**
41. 3 pieces chocolate (³⁄₄ oz/20 g in total) **13**

Large Snacks

200 calories in each snack
(two medium snacks = one large snack)
Total carbohydrate in grams is marked in red.

Mixed snacks

1. Vegetable and cracker bowl: 2 cups (500 mL) any kind of raw vegetables with 3 snackbreads, 2 bread sticks and 3 tbsp (45 mL) Vegetable Dip (page 189). **42**
2. 2 slices toast with 1 tsp (5 mL) butter or margarine and 2 tsp (10 mL) jam **38**
3. 1 cup (250 mL) cream of wheat hot cereal and ¾ cup (175 mL) low-fat milk **36**
4. 1 piece Crustless Pumpkin Pie (page 177) with 2 tbsp (25 mL) whipped topping **33**
5. 1 small cone with ¾ cup (175 mL) light ice cream **26**
6. 1 Bran Muffin (page 58) and ½ oz (15 g) cheese **29**
7. 1 piece Bannock (page 133) and 1 tsp (5 mL) jam **37**
8. 16 fresh peanuts **6**
9. 1 slice pumpernickel bread with 1 tsp (5 mL) margarine and 1½ oz (45 g) pickled herring **16**
10. 1 cup (250 mL) low-fat milk or buttermilk plus 3 plain cookies **30**
11. 1 cup (250 mL) Rice Pudding (page 129) **41**
12. 1 large cob of corn with 1 tsp (5 mL) butter or margarine **40**
13. 1 small baked potato with 1 tbsp (15 mL) light sour cream **47**
14. 1 Baked Apple (page 165) plus ½ oz (15 g) cheese **32**
15. 4 crackers with 2 large sardines **10**
16. ½ can cream of tomato soup made with low-fat milk, and 2 soda crackers **33**
17. 1 oz (30 g) cheese and asparagus on bread **16**
18. 1 shredded wheat biscuit with ½ small banana and ½ cup low-fat milk **45**
19. ½ bagel with 2 tbsp (25 mL) light cream cheese **27**

20. Mixed nuts as shown **7**
21. 16 baked tortilla chips and 2 tbsp (25 mL) hummus or salsa **26**
22. ham sandwich (1 oz/30 g) meat, no margarine) with mustard and lettuce **30**
23. 1 egg and 1 slice toast with 1 tsp (5 mL) margarine (1 tsp/5 mL jam is optional) **20**
24. 1 oz (30 g) cheese and fruit pieces **24**

Fruit

25. 2 fruits, such as a small apple and a pear **51**
26. ½ large avocado (try with a sprinkle of Worcestershire sauce or lemon) **8**

Occasional snacks

27. Small cake donut **23**
28. Cheesies (about 25) **20**
29. Potato chips (about 18) **18**
30. 1⅓-oz (40 g) chocolate bar **24**

Food Choices for Good Health

Does your shopping cart look like this?

This cart holds groceries for a week for two people, with many unhealthy food choices.

Compare this grocery cart to the healthier cart on page 289. You may be amazed by the difference.

Compared to the healthy cart on page 289, this cart has about:

- Eleven cups (2.75 L) of extra added table sugar — that's 513 teaspoons! This includes sugar added by the manufacturer to foods such as soft drinks, cookies, muffins, ice cream and chocolates. It also includes the sugar that comes from fruit juice.
- Half a pound (250 g), or 200 teaspoons (1 L), of extra fat. That would be like half a pound of butter.
- About 27,000 mg of extra sodium — as much as you would find in almost 12 teaspoons (60 mL) of salt.

Out with the old, in with the new.

Here are healthier food choices:

This cart holds groceries for a week for two people, with more healthy food choices. Compare this grocery cart to the unhealthier cart on page 288.

Compared to the unhealthy cart on page 288, this cart has:

- 486 g *more* fiber
- 450% *more* vitamin A
- 1,400% *more* vitamin C
- 410% *more* calcium

Rate your groceries!

Move from unhealthy to healthy choices using the charts on pages 291–317

Each page shows four different versions of a food or drink.

- The option at the top of the page is the least healthy.
- Generally, the bottom two choices are healthier than the top two choices.
- The bottom option, Karen's Choice, is what I consider the healthiest of the four possibilities.
- Keep in mind that nutrients differ among brands and sometimes between Canadian and American producers.

These charts are meant as a guideline only. When you're shopping, look carefully at food labels before deciding what to buy.

The following nutrients are listed for each food or drink:

- **Calories.** When you look at the calories in these charts, it's important to also consider the total amount of food you need each day. The small meals in this book provide about 1,200 calories per day and the large meals about 1,620 calories. Depending on your calorie requirements, you may be able to add 100 to 350 calories of snacks to the small meals and 100 to 600 calories of snacks to the large meals (see page 8).
- **Carbohydrates ("Carbs").** Carbs include starch from foods such as rice, wheat or pasta, the natural sugars found in fruits, vegetables and milk, and added sugar. One teaspoon (5 mL) of added sugar equals 4 g of sugar. Labels list the amount of sugar separately under carbohydrate, but this still gives no indication of how much is added sugar and how much is natural sugar. If the product is a soft drink, you'll know that all of the sugar is added sugar.
- **Fiber.** Fiber is very good for you, especially when you have diabetes. Adults with diabetes should eat 25 to 50 g of fiber a day.
- **Fat.** One teaspoon (5 mL) of butter, margarine, lard or oil has 5 g of fat. Fat should make up no more than one-third of your daily calories.
  - A daily meal plan of 1,200 calories a day should include no more than about 9 teaspoons (45 g) of fat, including hidden fat.
  - A daily meal plan of 1,620 calories a day should include no more than about 13 teaspoons (65 g) of fat, including hidden fat.
  Limit saturated fats and try to avoid trans fats. See page 41 for information about healthy fats.
- **Sodium.** It is best to limit your total sodium intake to 2,300 mg a day (about 1 teaspoon/5 mL of salt). This is often a challenge: most food products have salt added, sometimes large amounts.

Choosing the "healthiest" option (Karen's Choice) was often challenging, because one food product might be lower in sugar or fat (which is good) but higher in sodium or lower in fiber (not so good).

Caffeine content is listed only for food products that have more than 45 mg of caffeine. Because caffeine is an addictive drug, adults should limit it to 400 mg a day (300 mg if pregnant or breastfeeding). Children and teenagers should limit caffeine even more — or avoid it altogether.

Oatmeal

½ cup (125 mL) instant sweetened oatmeal (made from a 38-g package) with ½ cup (125 mL) 2% milk

Calories	Carbs	Fiber	Fat	Sodium
213	35 g	2 g	5 g	294 mg

These are super-sweetened packages of oatmeal. Cut back on the sugar by mixing half a package with plain oatmeal.

½ cup (125 mL) instant unsweetened (plain) oatmeal (made from a 28-g package) with ½ tsp (2 mL) brown sugar and ½ cup (125 mL) 2% milk

Calories	Carbs	Fiber	Fat	Sodium
171	26 g	3 g	4 g	274 mg

With 1 tsp (5 mL) brown sugar added, this still has less sugar than the presweetened package of oatmeal above.

¾ cup (175 mL) cooked minute oats with ½ tsp (2 mL) brown sugar and ½ cup (125 mL) 1% milk

Calories	Carbs	Fiber	Fat	Sodium
173	28 g	3 g	3 g	55 mg

Minute oats are healthier, as they have less sodium. They only take a few minutes longer to cook than the instant oats and can still be cooked in the microwave in your bowl.

1 cup (250 mL) old-fashioned oats with ½ tsp (2 mL) brown sugar and ½ cup (125 mL) skim milk

Calories	Carbs	Fiber	Fat	Sodium
180	31 g	4 g	2 g	53 mg

With homemade oatmeal you get "more" for about the same calories. Cook these oats on the stove or in the microwave. They are an excellent choice, as they raise your blood sugar a bit more slowly than minute oats and instant oats. When you choose skim milk, you have all the nutrients with no fat.

KAREN'S CHOICE

FOOD FACT ▶ Oats can help reduce your cholesterol. A low-calorie brown sugar substitute can be added to your oatmeal instead of sugar.

Cold Cereal

1½ cups (375 mL) granola crunch with ¾ cup (175 mL) 2% milk

Calories	Carbs	Fiber	Fat	Sodium
710	97 g	9 g	30 g	203 mg

Granola is an excellent source of fiber and is lower in sodium than other cereal choices, but it is very high in calories, sugar and saturated fat. Limit your serving to ¼ to ⅓ cup (50 to 75 mL), or use it as a topping on plain cereal.

1½ cups (375 mL) frosted flakes with ¾ cup (175 mL) 1% milk

Calories	Carbs	Fiber	Fat	Sodium
279	57 g	1 g	2 g	359 mg

Frosted flakes are high in sugar — 6 tsp (30 mL) of sugar have been added to this serving. Sugar-coated cereals are best sprinkled on top of your corn flakes or bran flakes.

1½ cups (375 mL) corn flakes with ¾ cup (175 mL) skim milk

Calories	Carbs	Fiber	Fat	Sodium
208	41 g	1 g	0 g	347 mg

Corn flakes have lower carbs and sodium than the other cereal choices in this chart. This makes them a good choice. However, they have little fiber. You could boost the fiber with a sprinkle of natural bran or bran buds on top.

1½ cups (375 mL) bran flakes with ¾ cup (175 mL) skim milk

Calories	Carbs	Fiber	Fat	Sodium
209	44 g	6 g	1 g	467 mg

Bran flakes are my choice because they are an excellent source of fiber. Yet compared to frosted flakes and corn flakes, they are higher in sodium. If reducing sodium is your priority, choose the corn flakes.

KAREN'S CHOICE

FOOD FACT Having a piece of fruit with your cereal adds healthy antioxidants and 2 to 5 g of fiber.

Milk

1 cup (250 mL) 2% chocolate milk

Calories	Carbs	Fiber	Fat	Sodium
180	26 g	1 g	5 g	150 mg

Chocolate milk has good nutrients, including calcium and vitamin D. To cut back on the added sugar, mix ½ cup (125 mL) chocolate milk with ½ cup (125 mL) skim milk. Your store may also sell 1% chocolate milk.

1 cup (250 mL) 3.3% (homogenized) milk

Calories	Carbs	Fiber	Fat	Sodium
146	11 g	0 g	8 g	98 mg

If you are used to drinking whole milk, try mixing it half and half with 2% milk. Eventually you may drink 2% milk and lower your fat intake.

1 cup (250 mL) 1% milk

Calories	Carbs	Fiber	Fat	Sodium
102	12 g	0 g	2 g	107 mg

This is a great lower-fat milk choice.

1 cup (250 mL) skim milk

Calories	Carbs	Fiber	Fat	Sodium
83	12 g	0 g	0	103 mg

Skim milk has zero fat. Plus, it has all the protein, calcium, vitamin D and other nutrients found in whole milk that are so important for your health. Try the delicious Fruit Milkshake on page 121.

KAREN'S CHOICE

FOOD FACT   A small glass of milk at the end of your meal can decrease the amount of acid in your mouth. This helps reduce the build-up of plaque on your teeth.

Restaurant Egg Breakfast

2 fried eggs, 2 slices of buttered white toast, 2 jams, 2 sausages, 1 cup (250 mL) hash browns, 1 tbsp (15 mL) ketchup, 20-oz (600 mL) coffee with 4 creamers (4 tbsp/60 mL) and 4 tsp (20 mL) sugar

Calories	Carbs	Fiber	Fat	Sodium
1,147	123 g	6 g	62 g	1,194 mg

This "breakfast special" gives you a whole day's fat intake. Save this meal for special occasions. (Note: 1 package of jam = 2 tsp/10 mL and 1 creamer = 1 tbsp/15 mL) **Caffeine: 343 mg** (based on filter drip).

2 poached eggs, 2 slices of buttered brown toast, 1 jam, 2 sausages, ½ cup (125 mL) hash browns, 10-oz (300 mL) coffee with 2 tbsp (25 mL) whole milk and 1 tsp (5 mL) sugar

Calories	Carbs	Fiber	Fat	Sodium
705	66 g	6 g	39 g	886 mg

Poached eggs, less jam on your toast and just one mug of coffee are good changes. You will eat less fat and sugar at one meal. **Caffeine: 171 mg.**

2 poached eggs, 2 slices of buttered brown toast, 1 jam, 2 sausages, tomato slices, 10-oz (300 mL) coffee with 2 tbsp (25 mL) whole milk

Calories	Carbs	Fiber	Fat	Sodium
530	43 g	5 g	30 g	862 mg

This breakfast replaces hash browns with tomato slices and cuts out almost 2 tsp (10 mL) of fat and more than 150 calories. **Caffeine: 171 mg.** (Switching to instant coffee reduces caffeine to about 114 mg.)

1 poached egg, 2 slices of unbuttered brown toast, 1 jam, tomato slices, 10-oz (300 mL) tea with 2 tbsp (25 mL) 2% milk

Calories	Carbs	Fiber	Fat	Sodium
286	42 g	5 g	8 g	480 mg

This is a trimmed-down, healthier breakfast. Choose a low-calorie sweetener for your tea (or coffee) if desired. **Caffeine: 59 mg.** (Decaf tea and most herbal teas have no caffeine.)

KAREN'S CHOICE

FOOD FACT Tea has almost three-quarters less caffeine than coffee. Plus, it is rich in antioxidants that may help keep your blood vessels healthy.

Jam

1 tbsp (15 mL) pure raspberry jam

Calories	Carbs	Fiber	Fat	Sodium
55	14 g	0 g	0 g	6 mg

One tablespoon (15 mL) of jam has the same amount of calories and total sugar as a piece of fresh fruit. However, jam does not have the fiber of fresh fruit, so it will raise your blood sugar faster.

1 tbsp (15 mL) "all-fruit" raspberry jam/spread, sweetened only with concentrated fruit juice

Calories	Carbs	Fiber	Fat	Sodium
50	12 g	0 g	0 g	0 mg

This sugar-free jam has similar amounts of calories and total sugar as regular jam (concentrated grape juice is like adding table sugar). When comparing labels, check the total carbohydrate, which includes the sugar from juice and table sugar.

1 tsp (5 mL) pure raspberry jam

Calories	Carbs	Fiber	Fat	Sodium
18	5 g	0 g	0 g	2 mg

Keep your portion of regular jam to 1 tsp (5 mL) per serving. This is about a thumbtip-size amount of jam.

1 tbsp (15 mL) no-sugar-added jam/spread (10 to 20 calories per tbsp/15 mL)

Calories	Carbs	Fiber	Fat	Sodium
10	2 g	0 g	0 g	5 mg

One tablespoon (15 mL) of this jam/spread has 10 to 20 calories. The lowest-calorie variety will be sweetened with a low-calorie sweetener, such as sucralose.

KAREN'S CHOICE

FOOD FACT | Some people find that eating 1 to 2 tsp (5 to 10 mL) of jam or honey helps satisfy a sugar craving.

Bagel Breakfast

1 large (4-inch/10 cm or 102 g) bagel (unbuttered) with 3 tbsp (45 mL) cream cheese, 20-oz (600 mL) coffee with 4 creamers (4 tbsp/60 mL) and 4 tsp (20 mL) sugar

Calories	Carbs	Fiber	Fat	Sodium
640	81 g	3 g	28 g	751 mg

Bagels are a dense type of bread. One 4-inch (10 cm) bagel has the same number of carbs as 4 slices of bread. **Caffeine: 448 mg** (based on filter drip).

1 large (4-inch/10 cm or 102 g) bagel (unbuttered) with 1 tbsp (15 mL) cream cheese, 10-oz (300 mL) coffee with 2 creamers (2 tbsp/25 mL) and 2 tsp (10 mL) sugar

Calories	Carbs	Fiber	Fat	Sodium
445	70 g	3 g	12 g	647 mg

Simply cutting back on the size of your coffee makes a big difference in the amount of cream and sugar you'll use. Small changes are easier than big changes. **Caffeine: 224 mg.**

1 small (3-inch/7.5 cm or 53 g) bagel (unbuttered) with 1 tbsp (15 mL) light cream cheese, 10-oz (300 mL) decaf coffee with 2 tbsp (25 mL) 2% milk

Calories	Carbs	Fiber	Fat	Sodium
206	33 g	1 g	4 g	367 mg

Here's a lighter choice! Not all coffee shops sell small bagels, but you can buy them at the grocery store, toast your bagel at home and add a smear of light cream cheese. **Caffeine: 4 mg.**

1 small (3-inch/7.5 cm or 53 g) bagel (unbuttered) with 1 tbsp (15 mL) sugar-free jam, 10-oz (300 mL) decaf coffee with 2 tbsp (25 mL) 2% milk

Calories	Carbs	Fiber	Fat	Sodium
192	37 g	1 g	1 g	323 mg

Switching from cream cheese to a sugar-free jam increases your carbs slightly but decreases total calories and fat. Low-calorie sweetener can be added to coffee or tea, if desired. **Caffeine: 4 mg.**

KAREN'S CHOICE

FOOD FACT Why does a bagel have a hole? Two reasons. The hole provides more even cooking and enabled traditional vendors to carry them on a string or stick.

Deli Sandwich

Rye bread, 2 thin large slices (2 oz/60 g) pastrami, 2 tsp (10 mL) mustard, 2 tsp (10 mL) butter, ¼ cup (50 mL) sauerkraut, 1 medium dill pickle

Calories	Carbs	Fiber	Fat	Sodium
330	35 g	6 g	14 g	2,101 mg

Did you notice the sodium? Save this sandwich for a special occasion only or choose one of the options below.

Rye bread, 1 thin slice (1 oz/30 g) pastrami, 2 tsp (10 mL) mustard, 2 tsp (10 mL) butter, 1 medium dill pickle

Calories	Carbs	Fiber	Fat	Sodium
286	33 g	5 g	12 g	1,515 mg

If you are buying a pastrami rye sandwich at a restaurant, ask the server to hold the sauerkraut. This helps reduce the sodium.

Rye bread, 1 thin slice (1 oz/30 g) pastrami, 2 tsp (10 mL) mustard, 1 medium dill pickle

Calories	Carbs	Fiber	Fat	Sodium
218	33 g	5 g	4 g	1,461 mg

To cut calories and sodium further, ask for your bread to be unbuttered. If you use home-cooked sliced roast beef, turkey or chicken, the sodium is even further reduced.

Rye bread, 1 thin slice (1 oz/30 g) pastrami, 1 tsp (5 mL) mustard, lettuce, tomato, ½ medium dill pickle

Calories	Carbs	Fiber	Fat	Sodium
215	33 g	5 g	4 g	1,119 mg

This reduced-salt version still contains almost half of the suggested daily intake of sodium. So make sure not to have luncheon meat on a daily basis, or use your own home-cooked sliced roast beef, turkey or chicken.

KAREN'S CHOICE

FOOD FACT

When buying bread, look for thinner or smaller slices that have about 70 to 80 calories per slice.

Cream Soup

Half of a 10-oz (284 mL) can of condensed cream of tomato soup, made with an equal amount of 3.3% (homogenized) milk, 3½-oz (100 g) tea biscuit with 2 tsp (10 mL) butter

Calories	Carbs	Fiber	Fat	Sodium
617	76 g	3 g	30 g	2,031 mg

The extra fat in this meal comes from the whole milk in the soup and the butter on the biscuit.

Half of a 10-oz (284 mL) can of condensed cream of tomato soup, made with an equal amount of 2% milk, 3½-oz (100 g) tea biscuit with 1 tsp (5 mL) butter

Calories	Carbs	Fiber	Fat	Sodium
568	76 g	3 g	24 g	2,006 mg

The switch to 2% milk cuts some calories and fat.

Half of a 10-oz (284 mL) can of condensed reduced-sodium cream of tomato soup, made with an equal amount of skim milk, 3½-oz (100 g) tea biscuit (unbuttered)

Calories	Carbs	Fiber	Fat	Sodium
523	77 g	2 g	19 g	1,679 mg

When you switch to skim milk, you reduce the calories and fat further. Choosing a reduced-sodium soup can cut salt by 20% to 30%, depending on the brand. Low-sodium varieties reduce the sodium even more, but are more difficult to find.

Half of a 10-oz (284 mL) can of condensed reduced-sodium cream of tomato soup, made with an equal amount of skim milk, 6 unsalted soda crackers, veggies

Calories	Carbs	Fiber	Fat	Sodium
262	47 g	3 g	5 g	805 mg

For an even lighter choice, switch to soda crackers and veggies on the side.

KAREN'S CHOICE

FOOD FACT Boil meat or poultry bones for a great soup stock. Add onions and herbs, leftover vegetables and some barley or noodles for a tasty low-salt soup.

Chicken Leg

1 drumstick and thigh, with skin, breaded and deep-fried

Calories	Carbs	Fiber	Fat	Sodium
360	12 g	0 g	21 g	368 mg

One piece of deep-fried chicken never hurt anyone. But eating fried chicken every day is a health risk. Fried chicken tends to be eaten with other high-fat foods, including fries, gravy and coleslaw laden with high-fat mayonnaise.

1 drumstick and thigh, with skin, coated with commercial crumb coating and baked

Calories	Carbs	Fiber	Fat	Sodium
286	4 g	0 g	19 g	234 mg

Here's a lower-fat homemade alternative using commercial crumb coating (such as Shake'n Bake™) for the chicken.

1 drumstick and thigh, skin removed, coated with commercial crumb coating and baked

Calories	Carbs	Fiber	Fat	Sodium
173	4 g	0 g	7 g	217 mg

Remove the skin from the chicken and you remove 2½ tsp (12 mL) of fat for this serving. This is still a delicious alternative.

1 drumstick and thigh, skin removed, coated with salt-free spice blend and baked

Calories	Carbs	Fiber	Fat	Sodium
148	0 g	0 g	6 g	80 mg

This choice reduces the calories and sodium by using the low-cost homemade Chicken Spice Mix on page 112. You can also use a commercial low-salt spice blend.

KAREN'S CHOICE

FOOD FACT By baking the chicken at home, you're not only making an awesome healthy change, but you're also saving money!

299

Fish

Store-bought frozen breaded white fish (5 oz/150 g), baked

Calories	Carbs	Fiber	Fat	Sodium
308	28 g	1 g	13 g	814 mg

Because of the heavy breading, this choice is highest in both carbs and sodium, and contains the least amount of fish — only 2 oz (30 g). If you are eating at home, choose the "healthy bake" type of frozen fish and have a salad, vegetables and oven-baked fries (see page 156).

White fish (5 oz/150 g), battered and deep-fried

Calories	Carbs	Fiber	Fat	Sodium
329	24 g	1 g	17 g	754 mg

This 5-oz (150 g) choice has 2 oz (60 g) of batter and only 3 oz (90 g) of fish). It is also a poor nutritional choice, as it is high in fat, especially saturated fat. In a restaurant, the fish would typically be served with french fries, further increasing the calories and fat in the meal.

White fish (5 oz/150 g), fried, broiled or baked with 1 tsp (5 mL) added fat

Calories	Carbs	Fiber	Fat	Sodium
193	0 g	0 g	5 g	151 mg

In the last two choices, you get a full 5 oz (150 g) of fish! Quickly cook up your fish in a teaspoon (5 mL) of fat (oil, butter or margarine) in a nonstick frying pan. Or bake it in the oven with the small amount of fat. Try Dinner 3 (page 120).

White fish (5 oz/150 g), broiled or steamed with dill or ¼ tsp (1 mL) pesto

Calories	Carbs	Fiber	Fat	Sodium
159	0 g	0 g	1 g	113 mg

A great way to cook white fish without fat is to wrap it in foil or parchment paper, then bake it. You may want to add chopped vegetables and basil or garlic. Pesto (a combination of basil, garlic and olive oil) can be bought ready-to-use in a squeeze tube.

KAREN'S CHOICE

FOOD FACT Fish is an excellent source of omega-3 fats, which keep your blood vessels healthy. Eating fish twice a week gives you all the omega-3s you need.

Fast-Food Burger with All Toppings

Third-pound burger (4 oz/112 g cooked weight) with double cheese and bacon

Calories	Carbs	Fiber	Fat	Sodium
780	53 g	3 g	44 g	1,990 mg

Restaurant burgers have layers of tasty ingredients, and that's reflected in the calories, fat and sodium. If you have fries and a drink with this burger, the fat and calories go up even higher.

Two single burgers (each burger = 1 oz/28 g cooked) with cheese and middle bun

Calories	Carbs	Fiber	Fat	Sodium
540	44 g	3 g	29 g	1,020 mg

This is a reduction but still pretty loaded. Know what you are eating: check out the calories and nutrients of the fast-food item online before you go out to eat, or ask for the nutrient brochure at the restaurant.

Cheeseburger (1 oz/28 g cooked weight burger) with bacon

Calories	Carbs	Fiber	Fat	Sodium
340	34 g	2 g	15 g	910 mg

This option has significantly less calories, fat and sodium. It's a good alternative and still tastes great!

Cheeseburger (1 oz/28 g cooked weight burger)

Calories	Carbs	Fiber	Fat	Sodium
300	33 g	2 g	12 g	750 mg

Of the four options here, this is the best choice when you're eating at a fast-food restaurant. Instead of choosing the meal deal, order individual items from the menu. Ask for a small fries or a salad on the side, and have milk instead of a soft drink. Alternatively, try Dinner 26 (page 212).

KAREN'S CHOICE

FOOD FACT It may seem like a waste not to get the meal deal, but remember: all those extra calories go to *your* waist.

Restaurant Pizza

3 pieces of thick-crust 12-inch (30 cm) deluxe pizza (with 6 pieces per pizza)

Calories	Carbs	Fiber	Fat	Sodium
1,659	143 g	7 g	87 g	3,474 mg

This option has the same number of calories as a large breakfast, lunch and dinner meal in this book combined — all in just three pieces of pizza! This serving has a whopping 1½ tsp (7 mL) of salt and more than a day's worth of fat.

3 pieces of thin-crust 12-inch (30 cm) deluxe pizza (with 6 pieces per pizza)

Calories	Carbs	Fiber	Fat	Sodium
1,346	91 g	7 g	81 g	2,757 mg

Cut carbs significantly by switching to thin-crust pizza. To help fill you up, drink water and have a salad or a half plate of your favorite cooked vegetables with your pizza.

2 pieces of thick-crust 12-inch (30 cm) pizza with two toppings, salad with a light dressing

Calories	Carbs	Fiber	Fat	Sodium
944	95 g	4 g	46 g	2,114 mg

To cut calories, fat and sodium, choose a pizza with fewer toppings. For pizza ideas, see Dinner 25 (page 208).

2 pieces of thin-crust 12-inch (30 cm) pizza with two toppings, salad with a light dressing

Calories	Carbs	Fiber	Fat	Sodium
782	65 g	4 g	44 g	1,742 mg

Add some extra vegetables to your pizza. Some of my favorite toppings are onions, asparagus, peppers, mushrooms, fresh tomatoes, sun-dried tomatoes and zucchini. Even this choice is salty, so it's best to not choose it every week.

KAREN'S CHOICE

FOOD FACT Slowing down your eating can help you eat less. Eat some vegetables or salad before your pizza, and drink water before and with your meal.

Ready-to-Serve Noodles

Noodles in a bowl, chicken flavor (110 g dry weight)

Calories	Carbs	Fiber	Fat	Sodium
481	70 g	3 g	17 g	2,278 mg

This product has a shocking amount of salt. Studies show that people with diabetes are not able to get rid of excess sodium as efficiently as people without diabetes. Eating too much sodium can worsen high blood pressure.

Noodles in a cup, chicken flavor (64 g dry weight)

Calories	Carbs	Fiber	Fat	Sodium
280	41 g	2 g	10 g	1,325 mg

The cup serving is smaller than the bowl and so has less sodium. However, this serving is still high in sodium.

Noodles in a cup, chicken flavor (64 g dry weight), made with half the spice mix

Calories	Carbs	Fiber	Fat	Sodium
274	39 g	1 g	10 g	776 mg

Here's an easy change to cut the salt in half: only add half the package of spice mix! To boost flavor, add some low-salt seasoning, such as Mrs. Dash or McCormick no-salt seasonings.

Noodles in a cup (64 g dry weight) without the chicken flavor mix, made instead with 1 tsp (5 mL) salt-free spice blend (or fresh herbs and/or chili or black pepper)

Calories	Carbs	Fiber	Fat	Sodium
268	37 g	1 g	10 g	226 mg

Are you ready to replace the whole package of spice mix with a low-salt seasoning or some tasty fresh herbs? You'll still enjoy the noodles, and you'll no longer have to worry about all that added salt.

KAREN'S CHOICE

FOOD FACT A noodle bowl is the carb equivalent of about 5 slices of bread and a noodle cup is equivalent to almost 3 slices of bread.

Potatoes

1 large serving (6 oz/175 g) fast-food french fries

Calories	Carbs	Fiber	Fat	Sodium
560	74 g	6 g	27 g	430 mg

The total fat in a serving of french fries is a concern if they're eaten regularly or daily. Also of concern is that fat heated to a high temperature in a deep-fryer changes into an unhealthy type of fat.

1 large serving (6 oz/175 g) baked frozen french fries, unsalted

Calories	Carbs	Fiber	Fat	Sodium
350	55 g	6 g	13 g	53 mg

Bake these lower-fat fries at home and serve them as part of a meal.

1 large baked potato with no added fat, with 2 tbsp (25 mL) fat-free sour cream, 1 tsp (5 mL) butter or margarine, and chopped green onion

Calories	Carbs	Fiber	Fat	Sodium
298	61 g	5 g	4 g	92 mg

As an alternative to fries, try a baked potato. The life-size photo that accompanies Dinner 1 (page 114) shows the size of 1½ medium potatoes (equivalent to 1 large potato). The carbs are a bit higher in this choice because of the toppings.

1 large potato, cut into sticks, tossed in 1 tsp (5 mL) oil and baked

Calories	Carbs	Fiber	Fat	Sodium
276	55 g	5 g	5 g	17 mg

This is a delicious and easy way to make home-baked fries. To spice them up, sprinkle on flavorings such as dried dillweed, chili powder or a commercial salt-free spice blend.

KAREN'S CHOICE

FOOD FACT ▶ **Potatoes are an excellent source of vitamin C and potassium.**

Vegetables

Deep-fried onion rings (medium order, 160 g)

Calories	Carbs	Fiber	Fat	Sodium
501	51 g	4 g	29 g	832 mg

The benefit of the onion (or other vegetable) is lost underneath the battering and frying, so please don't count this deep-fried snack as one of your "vegetables" for the day! The onions are now high in calories, fat and salt.

1½ cups (375 mL) mixed vegetables with ¼ cup (50 mL) cheese sauce, made with skim milk

Calories	Carbs	Fiber	Fat	Sodium
155	18 g	4 g	6 g	221 mg

To make cheese sauce for four: In a small saucepan, over medium heat, heat up 1 tbsp (15 mL) fat with 1 tbsp (15 mL) flour until small bubbles form. Add 1 cup (250 mL) skim milk and ½ cup (125 mL) shredded low-fat cheese. Stir with a whisk until smooth and thickened.

1½ cups (375 mL) mixed vegetables with 1 tsp (5 mL) margarine or butter

Calories	Carbs	Fiber	Fat	Sodium
95	13 g	4 g	5 g	105 mg

Choose a big serving of vegetables to help fill you up at your meal — you will find that you eat less meat and potatoes.

1½ cups (375 mL) mixed vegetables, lightly steamed, with herbs

Calories	Carbs	Fiber	Fat	Sodium
63	13 g	4 g	1 g	72 mg

Add ground pepper or fresh or dried herbs to your vegetables. This makes them tasty and enjoyable to eat.

KAREN'S CHOICE

FOOD FACT Onions and garlic, eaten raw or cooked, are excellent choices, as they may play a role in reducing blood clots.

Caesar Salad

Restaurant Caesar salad: 4 cups (1 L) romaine lettuce, ¼ cup (50 mL) Caesar salad dressing, ¼ cup (50 mL) croutons and 2 tbsp (25 mL) Parmesan cheese, plus 2 pieces of garlic bread

Calories	Carbs	Fiber	Fat	Sodium
798	58 g	8 g	57 g	1,564 mg

Many are surprised that a large Caesar salad from a restaurant has as many calories as a large burger. The reason is that Caesar salad dressing is mostly oil and is high in fat. Topped off with the garlic bread, this salad is not light!

Restaurant Caesar salad: 4 cups (1 L) romaine lettuce, ¼ cup (50 mL) Caesar salad dressing, ¼ cup (50 mL) croutons and 2 tbsp (25 mL) Parmesan cheese

Calories	Carbs	Fiber	Fat	Sodium
442	16 g	5 g	40 g	967 mg

To avoid the extra calories, ask the waiter not to bring out the garlic bread.

Restaurant Caesar salad: 4 cups (1 L) romaine lettuce, 2 tbsp (25 mL) Caesar salad dressing, ¼ cup (50 mL) croutons and 1 tbsp (15 mL) Parmesan cheese

Calories	Carbs	Fiber	Fat	Sodium
263	15 g	5 g	21 g	554 mg

Ask for a small amount of salad dressing on the side and limit your serving of dressing to 2 tbsp (25 mL). Some restaurants have an option for a light salad dressing.

Homemade Caesar salad: 4 cups (1 L) romaine lettuce, 1 tbsp (15 mL) light Caesar salad dressing, ¼ cup (50 mL) croutons and 1 tbsp (15 mL) Parmesan cheese

Calories	Carbs	Fiber	Fat	Sodium
125	17 g	5 g	5 g	400 mg

Simple and fast to prepare at home, this light salad choice makes a terrific appetizer or meal accompaniment. Light salad dressing is higher in salt, so you might choose to use regular salad dressing instead.

KAREN'S CHOICE

FOOD FACT Dark green lettuce, such as romaine, is rich in folate, which is helpful for your blood cholesterol.

Yogurt

¾ cup (175 mL) 6% fruit yogurt, sweetened with sugar

Calories	Carbs	Fiber	Fat	Sodium
240	29 g	0 g	11 g	98 mg

This high-fat yogurt has double the fat of a homogenized milk. Some other yogurts have extra fermenting bacteria added and are labeled as better for you. But look at the label, because they may be made with a higher-fat milk or extra sugar. They may not be the right choice for you.

¾ cup (175 mL) 3% frozen yogurt

Calories	Carbs	Fiber	Fat	Sodium
150	29 g	0 g	3 g	90 mg

Frozen yogurt is a nice dessert choice and has fewer calories than the high-fat yogurt above. It has similar calories to a 2% sweetened fruit yogurt.

¾ cup (175 mL) fat-free (0% fat) fruit yogurt, sweetened with sugar

Calories	Carbs	Fiber	Fat	Sodium
173	35 g	0 g	0 g	107 mg

This is a better choice because there's no fat, but there is still added sugar.

¾ cup (175 mL) fat-free (0% fat) fruit yogurt, sweetened with a low-calorie sweetener, plus ½ cup (125 mL) blueberries or other fresh or frozen fruit

Calories	Carbs	Fiber	Fat	Sodium
128	24 g	2 g	0 g	109 mg

By choosing a fat-free yogurt sweetened with a low-calorie sweetener, you avoid extra fat and added sugar. Like all yogurts, it contains natural sugar (carbohydrate) from the milk.

KAREN'S CHOICE

FOOD FACT

Yogurt is perhaps the oldest fermented milk product. There are records of its use dating back 2,500 years!

Ice Cream

3 scoops (each ½ cup/125 mL) of vanilla ice cream with ¼ cup (50 mL) chocolate sauce and 2 tbsp (25 mL) nuts (strawberry garnish)

Calories	Carbs	Fiber	Fat	Sodium
728	99 g	3 g	36 g	203 mg

This ice cream with toppings has as much fat and calories as a large fast-food burger (see page 301). This may not be the best choice for you.

3 scoops (each ½ cup/125 mL) of vanilla ice cream (strawberry garnish)

Calories	Carbs	Fiber	Fat	Sodium
442	53 g	2 g	24 g	173 mg

One or two scoops of ice cream in an ice cream cone would have less calories, carbs and fat than the three scoops of regular-fat ice cream. A standard cone has only 20 calories and can make the dessert seem more filling than when the ice cream is served in a bowl.

2 scoops (each ½ cup/125 mL) of vanilla ice cream (strawberry garnish)

Calories	Carbs	Fiber	Fat	Sodium
293	35 g	1 g	16 g	116 mg

If you put your ice cream in a bowl, remember to use a small bowl, to make it seem like more (see page 253). This may help you cut down to one scoop.

1 scoop (½ cup/125 mL) of vanilla ice cream with 1 cup (250 mL) strawberries or other fresh fruit

Calories	Carbs	Fiber	Fat	Sodium
198	30 g	4 g	8 g	59 mg

A half cup (125 mL) of ice cream has about the same calories as a ¾-cup (175 mL) serving of yogurt, but has less calcium. Adding fruit helps fill you up.

KAREN'S CHOICE

FOOD FACT Check labels: some ice creams are slightly lower in fat, sugar or calories.

Cookies

Two large (3½-inch/8.5 cm, 114 g) fast-food chocolate chunk cookies

Calories	Carbs	Fiber	Fat	Sodium
460	70 g	2 g	18 g	520 mg

It's probably a good idea to buy only one of these large cookies — but remember, even one has 230 calories, which is more than a large snack (see pages 284–285).

Three 2¼-inch (5.5 cm) commercial chocolate chunk cookies

Calories	Carbs	Fiber	Fat	Sodium
255	35 g	2 g	12 g	203 mg

Do you remember the cookies your grandmother used to make? Three of them have less carbs and calories than the two super-sized cookies above.

Three 2½-inch (6 cm) commercial chocolate chip cookies ("Dad's cookies")

Calories	Carbs	Fiber	Fat	Sodium
195	24 g	0 g	9 g	135 mg

Check the Nutrition Facts table on store-bought cookies, and avoid those with any amount of trans fat.

Three 2½-inch (6 cm) thin chocolate cookies

Calories	Carbs	Fiber	Fat	Sodium
98	14 g	1 g	4 g	98 mg

When you buy cookies, look for ones that are thinner and smaller, with less than 100 calories, 20 g of carbohydrates and 5 g of fat per 2 cookies.

KAREN'S CHOICE

FOOD FACT — **Try not to eat more than two or three small cookies for a dessert or snack. Substitute fruit for cookies more of the time.**

Muffin or Donut

Large blueberry bran muffin (128 g)

Calories	Carbs	Fiber	Fat	Sodium
380	58 g	5 g	15 g	530 mg

A common misconception is that coffee shop muffins (especially low-fat ones) are healthier than donuts. This is false because the muffins are made so large, they end up having more sugar and fat than standard-size donuts.

Cake donut (60 g) or cream-filled donut (89 g)

Calories	Carbs	Fiber	Fat	Sodium
253	30 g	1 g	14 g	328 mg

Many coffee shops have the nutrient information of their muffins, donuts and other foods and drinks listed online. If you eat at one regularly, compare the nutrient listings.

3 donut "holes" (50 to 55 g total)

Calories	Carbs	Fiber	Fat	Sodium
219	26 g	1 g	12 g	284 mg

For a lighter donut choice with your coffee or tea, choose two or three donut "holes."

Homemade Bran Muffin (see recipe, page 58)

Calories	Carbs	Fiber	Fat	Sodium
144	29 g	4 g	3 g	234 mg

Commercial muffin mixes come in low-fat varieties. Compare the nutrient information to this muffin. Although this choice appears to have more carbs than the 3 donut holes, the available carb is less. It is an excellent source of fiber and is low in fat.

KAREN'S CHOICE

FOOD FACT The size of the muffin determines the total amount of sugar and fat. Bigger muffins can have similar amounts of sugar and fat as donuts.

Apple Dessert

1 piece of homemade double-crust apple pie (¹⁄₆th of a 9-inch/23 cm pie), made with 5 apples

Calories	Carbs	Fiber	Fat	Sodium
556	71 g	3 g	29 g	517 mg

Enjoy apple pie just occasionally. Once you add a double crust to a pie, it's like adding 4 slices of buttered bread to your fruit filling. Ice cream on top of your pie will add more sugar and fat.

³⁄₄ cup (175 mL) traditional apple crisp (¹⁄₆ of recipe, see below)

Calories	Carbs	Fiber	Fat	Sodium
314	55 g	2 g	11 g	378 mg

Recipe includes 5 apples, ³⁄₄ cup (175 mL) flour, 1 cup (250 mL) brown sugar, ³⁄₄ tsp (3 mL) salt, 1 tsp (5 mL) ground cinnamon and ¹⁄₃ cup (75 mL) butter or margarine. Using a topping rather than a crust cuts the calories and fat.

³⁄₄ cup (175 mL) healthier apple crisp (¹⁄₆ of recipe, see below)

Calories	Carbs	Fiber	Fat	Sodium
224	37 g	3 g	9 g	62 mg

Recipe includes 5 apples, ¹⁄₄ cup (50 mL) whole wheat flour, ¹⁄₂ cup (125 mL) rolled oats, ¹⁄₂ cup (125 mL) brown sugar, 1 tsp (5 mL) ground cinnamon and ¹⁄₄ cup (50 mL) butter or margarine. If you want, you could replace some of the brown sugar with a low-calorie sweetener.

1 Baked Apple (see recipe, page 165)

Calories	Carbs	Fiber	Fat	Sodium
141	32 g	3 g	3 g	23 mg

You can still satisfy your sweet tooth with this choice, which has fewer calories and less fat and sugar.

KAREN'S CHOICE

FOOD FACT Adding cinnamon to desserts and cereals helps replace some of the sweetening, so you don't need to add as much sugar.

Canned or Fresh Fruit

Two half peaches in syrup

Calories	Carbs	Fiber	Fat	Sodium
145	39 g	3 g	0 g	12 mg

By rinsing the fruit in water, you can remove some of the extra sugar added during the canning process.

Two half peaches in juice

Calories	Carbs	Fiber	Fat	Sodium
86	23 g	3 g	0 g	8 mg

Switching to juice-packed instead of syrup-packed fruit is an easy way to cut calories and carbs. Most stores sell juice-packed fruit for the same price as the syrup-packed fruit.

Two half peaches in water

Calories	Carbs	Fiber	Fat	Sodium
47	12 g	3 g	0 g	6 mg

As fresh peaches are seasonal, these canned peaches make an excellent alternative. The label may say "no sugar added." Unfortunately, peaches canned in water are not always available or may be more expensive.

1 fresh peach (medium-large)

Calories	Carbs	Fiber	Fat	Sodium
50	12 g	3 g	0 g	0 mg

When peaches are in season, go with the fresh fruit. A fresh peach has similar nutrients as peaches canned in water. Calories and carbs vary slightly depending on the size of the peach.

KAREN'S CHOICE

FOOD FACT Chinese kings and emperors used to consider peaches an exquisite delight — now everyone can eat like a king!

Cheese and Crackers

1½ oz (45 g) regular-fat cheese plus 6 party crackers (20 g)

Calories	Carbs	Fiber	Fat	Sodium
271	13 g	0 g	19 g	464 mg

Do party crackers tempt you to overeat? If so, keep them as a "party treat," not an everyday choice.

1½ oz (45 g) regular-fat cheese plus 6 reduced-sodium (61% less sodium) party crackers (20 g)

Calories	Carbs	Fiber	Fat	Sodium
271	14 g	1 g	19 g	334 mg

An easy way to reduce salt is to look for low-sodium crackers. Salt is used to preserve cheeses, so low-sodium cheeses don't store as well and are harder to find.

1 oz (30 g) regular-fat cheese plus 4 whole-grain crackers (18 g)

Calories	Carbs	Fiber	Fat	Sodium
194	13 g	2 g	12 g	291 mg

In this choice, four whole-grain crackers replace the six party-type crackers. You can have this option as a snack or incorporate it into your lunch meal (see Lunch 13, page 102).

1 oz (30 g) regular-fat cheese plus 4 reduced-sodium (61% less sodium) whole-grain crackers (18 g)

Calories	Carbs	Fiber	Fat	Sodium
194	13 g	2 g	12 g	221 mg

Whole-grain and whole wheat crackers are both good choices. Unfortunately, not all whole wheat crackers are available unsalted. For example, you can buy unsalted plain soda crackers, but whole wheat soda crackers are salted.

KAREN'S CHOICE

FOOD FACT   **Light Cheddar cheese has less than 20% milk fat (M.F.).**

Popcorn

Large buttered movie theater popcorn (20 cups/5 L with 6 pumps of butter, equal to 3 tbsp/45 mL)

Calories	Carbs	Fiber	Fat	Sodium
1,405	126 g	22 g	96 g	2,190 mg

The amount of fat and salt in this super-sized serving might be enough to scare you or make you cry, if the movie doesn't.

Small buttered movie theater popcorn (7 cups/1.75 L with 3 pumps of butter, equal to 1½ tbsp/22 mL)

Calories	Carbs	Fiber	Fat	Sodium
538	44 g	8 g	39 g	803 mg

Studies have been done where people were given very stale popcorn at a movie theater, and they still ate it all. If you want to eat less, buy a smaller serving.

4 cups (1 L) home-popped popcorn, made with 1 tsp (5 mL) oil for ¼ cup (50 mL) kernels, plus 3 shakes of salt (¹⁄₁₆ tsp/0.25 mL)

Calories	Carbs	Fiber	Fat	Sodium
164	24 g	4 g	6 g	147 mg

A better choice. It contains about half the fat and sodium of the same amount of movie theater popcorn. Try peanut oil for a great flavor! Electric popcorn makers with motorized stirring rods make yummy popcorn with little oil.

4 cups (1 L) air-popped popcorn

Calories	Carbs	Fiber	Fat	Sodium
122	25 g	4 g	1 g	1 mg

Popcorn can be air-popped with an electric air popper or a microwave popcorn popper.

KAREN'S CHOICE

FOOD FACT   Popcorn is believed to have been discovered by Native Americans over 5,000 years ago when corn was being cooked over the open fire.

Juice or Soft Drink

12 oz (341 mL) unsweetened apple juice

Calories	Carbs	Fiber	Fat	Sodium
168	42 g	0 g	0 g	11 mg

Even unsweetened fruit juice has a lot of natural sugar; in fact, some juices have more total sugar than some soft drinks. It's easy to drink a lot of sugar quickly. Note too that juice has very little fiber, so it does not replace fresh fruit. (Note: a 12-oz/341 mL beverage bottle or can contains about 1½ cups.)

12 oz (341 mL) cola

Calories	Carbs	Fiber	Fat	Sodium
155	40 g	0 g	0 g	15 mg

Regular cola is high in added sugar and caffeine. If you drink a 2-quart (2 L) bottle of cola, you get 53 tsp (265 mL) of sugar and 200 to 300 mg of caffeine. Energy drinks can have double or more of this amount of caffeine. **Caffeine: 36–46 mg.**

12 oz (341 mL) diet cola

Calories	Carbs	Fiber	Fat	Sodium
4	1 g	0 g	0 g	18 mg

With zero sugar, this is the preferred choice over regular cola. However, diet cola, like regular cola, is high in caffeine, and all colas have acids that can damage your teeth. Cola also has phosphates that, when consumed daily, can weaken your bones. **Caffeine: 39–50 mg.**

12 oz (341 mL) water

Calories	Carbs	Fiber	Fat	Sodium
0 g	0 g	0 g	0 g	11 mg

Water is the best choice! Fluoridated tap water can help keep your teeth strong.

KAREN'S CHOICE

FOOD FACT ▸ **All unsweetened juices have a lot of natural sugar, so limit yourself to a ½-cup (125 mL) glass or choose a fresh fruit instead.**

Chocolate and Nut Snacks

Super-sized (300 g) milk chocolate and nut bar

Calories	Carbs	Fiber	Fat	Sodium
1,620	180 g	12 g	96 g	120 mg

Some box stores now carry super-sized chocolate bars. If you are a chocolate fanatic and you buy one of these, you may eat the whole thing in a day or two. Avoid the temptation by leaving it on the store shelf.

Large (100 g) milk chocolate and nut bar

Calories	Carbs	Fiber	Fat	Sodium
522	55 g	2 g	35 g	69 mg

This is a smaller bar than the one above, but still has a whopping 522 calories. It's better to keep large chocolate bars out of sight and out of mind by not buying them in the first place.

Standard-size (43 g) milk chocolate and nut bar

Calories	Carbs	Fiber	Fat	Sodium
240	22 g	1 g	15 g	30 mg

You can fit an "old-fashioned"-sized chocolate bar into your "treat budget." Enjoy one on occasion and don't feel guilty about it.

10 almonds and 2 small pieces (20 g total weight) of dark chocolate (80% cacao)

Calories	Carbs	Fiber	Fat	Sodium
176	6 g	3 g	15 g	7 mg

This small serving of almonds, along with a small amount of chocolate, would fit into the large snack group (pages 284–285). Chocolate with at least 80% cacao is a good choice, as cacao has healthy antioxidants.

KAREN'S CHOICE

FOOD FACT Chocolate is known for its antioxidants. Cocoa powder (cacao) also contains these antioxidants, but is much lower in fat than chocolate.

Other "Special Treat" Snacks

Large (220 g) bag of potato chips (about 110 chips) with ½ cup (125 mL) commercial chip dip

Calories	Carbs	Fiber	Fat	Sodium
1,468	124 g	8 g	103 g	2,283 mg

You are distracted when you watch TV, so you might easily get all the way through this large bag of potato chips. It's shocking to learn that this serving contains the equivalent of about 4½ medium potatoes, 26 tsp (130 mL) of oil and more calories than some people need in an entire day.

Large (220 g) bag of cheese puffs or cheese twists (about 150)

Calories	Carbs	Fiber	Fat	Sodium
1,219	118 g	2 g	76 g	2,310 mg

Don't be fooled into thinking cheese puffs have any cheese in them! Like potato chips, they are mostly starch, fat and salt.

Half of a large (220 g) bag of potato chips (about 55 chips)

Calories	Carbs	Fiber	Fat	Sodium
614	56 g	4 g	42 g	722 mg

Cutting your portion of chips in half is a good change, as is skipping the dip. However, if you would like a dip with these chips, choose the Vegetable Dip or the low-salt Garlic Vegetable Dip on page 189.

Small (45 g) bag of potato chips (20 to 25 chips)

Calories	Carbs	Fiber	Fat	Sodium
241	22 g	2 g	16 g	240 mg

There are 20 to 25 chips in a bag this size, so if you have purchased a larger bag, try putting just that amount in a bowl for your snack.

KAREN'S CHOICE

FOOD FACT ▶ One potato chip has about 1 g of carbohydrate. If you eat 30 chips, it's like eating 2 slices of bread topped with 5 to 6 tsp (25 to 30 mL) of butter.

Index